C000156991

Stan the Man

The Life Story of Stan Wall, from Top Rugby League Referee to Super League's Most Famous Kitman

(Whilst Digging a Little Bit of Coal along the Way)

Stan Wall and Andrew Quirke

Vertical Editions

www.verticaleditions.com

Copyright © Stan Wall and Andrew Quirke 2014

The right of Eric Chisnall and Andrew Quirke to be identified
as the authors of this work has been asserted in accordance with
the Copyright, Designs and Patents Act, 1988

All rights reserved. The reproduction and utilisation of
this book in any form or by any electrical, mechanical or
other means, now known or hereafter invented, including
photocopying and recording, and in any information storage
and retrieval system, is forbidden without the written
permission of the publisher

First published in the United Kingdom in 2014 by Vertical
Editions, Unit 4a, Snaygill Industrial Estate, Skipton, North
Yorkshire BD23 2QR

www.verticaleditions.com

ISBN 978-1-904091-83-7

A CIP catalogue record for this book is available from the
British Library

Cover design by HBA, York

Printed and bound by CMP (uk) Ltd, Poole, Dorset

Contents

Stan's Dedication

For my dear wife Celia, my children Sharon and Dean, my grandchildren Garry, Nicola, Craig and Lauren, and my great grandchildren Aaron, Oliver, Tom and Coby.

Andrew's Dedication

For my son Oliver and also for my Gran and Granddad who are no longer with us but I think would have loved this especially Stan's early memories.

Andrew's Thanks

First and foremost, thanks to Ste Leonard who once again lined this one up for me.

A big thanks to Stan Wall for allowing me to work on his life story with him. Stan put a tremendous amount of hard work into this book; sorry for the sleepless nights mate! The energy and memory recall you have is sensational and I wish I had half of it. Also thanks to Stan's wife Celia for being so welcoming and all the cups of tea we drank whilst this was put together.

Thanks to Karl Waddicor at Vertical Editions.

A big thanks to Catherine Taylor for very kindly proofing the initial draft of this book.

Thanks to Sean Long for the foreword.

Thanks to Bernard Platt for the photos of Stan at St Helens.

Thanks to the following for providing me with contacts during the writing of this book: Andy Wilson, Phil Wilkinson, Mike Critchley, Mike Appleton, Jeff Boardman, Phil Clarke and Yannick Rey at the Catalans Dragons.

Thanks to everyone who agreed to be interviewed.

Finaly, thanks to the following for all your support as ever: my mum, Kevin, Paul, Mike and Chris (the boys), Paul Bennett, Fiee Shiel, Niccy Shiel Kieran, Nicola Perks, Graham Wilson, Kate Wilkinson, Caron Campbell, Ste Radford, Ben and Tereska Leach, Julia Ryan, Ben Smithurst and finally because I promised him I would, Tony Jackson.

Ex Terra Lucem

Foreword by Sean Long

I'd just signed for St Helens on the Thursday and at first, it had to be kept quiet. On the Saturday, we went for the team run. I got there and realised I had left all my gear at Widnes so had no boots. I went into the kit room where Stan was, introduced myself to him and he was dead nice. He had a nice stash of boots in the boot room. He got me some new Mizuno boots and some training kit. We got on like a house on fire straightaway.

We formed a partnership where I would come in early for training, go to his kitroom and have a brew with him.

Basically, Stan wiped our backsides, anything we wanted he got us. He didn't have to but he went out of his way for us. Our boots would be immaculate when we'd come to play and our kit would be laid out ready for us. Anything else we wanted he would make sure we were sorted. There'd be times I'd forget something and Stan would always look after me.

You don't realise what an important role people like Stan play at a club behind the scenes. He'd made sure that on game day you had nothing to worry about. All you had to do was go out and perform and play your game. You don't get that at other clubs. It was just Stan being the guy he is.

I'd be pretty pumped after we had scored a try and when you're kicking a goal you need to relax. He would come on with the kicking tee, I'd be hyper and he'd be telling me to take my time. I'd speak to him and get some feedback off him. I'd tell him which cloud in the sky I was aiming my kick for as I'd always aim higher than the sticks. He'd tell me where the wind was blowing. It made my feel really relaxed. Sometimes I'd miss, most of the times I'd get it. If I had missed, the next kick, Stan would tell me to relax and that I was rushing it. I'd have a minute, I just felt more relaxed with Stan coming on with the kicking tee. I kicked some quite important goals when Stan came on. A lot of the times – including Grand Finals – it was because Stan had calmed me down.

Stan was always in the club first, I was always one of the early players in so I would always have a chat with him. I'd get in around eight-ish in a morning for training at 10. Stan would be at the club shortly after half six every morning. One day, I came into the dressing room nearest Stan's room to see Stan stood there in his undies on a little pair of stepladders painting the dressing room. The heating was on full whack, I don't know why. He was just stood there painting in his undies. I thought 'what is going on here'. I couldn't get my head around it to be honest so put the kettle on and had a brew. A normal kitman would just be dealing with the boots. Here was Stan painting the dressing rooms nearly in the knack. It was hardly a sight for sore eyes, he looked like Gandhi with a paint brush. That's one good memory amongst many I have of Stan.

I can't wait for Stan's story to be told. Every time I had a brew and a chat with him, Joynty and Newy on a morning before training, he would always tell us some tales of mining, refereeing or coaching. Every tale would be different. I just used to sit there and listen to him for an hour; I found it quite relaxing. Now this book is out, it will be good to read those stories again; I know there's plenty of good ones.

Introduction

I remember as a little kid my favourite book was without doubt the *Rothmans Rugby League Yearbook*. It contained a review of the season just gone and a guide to every club in the game. Such was my enthusiasm for the sport, I could tell you the name of each professional club's ground and their nickname back in those days. I wouldn't have a clue if I attempted it now.

Many of the books I have worked on centre on personalities who were prevalent in the 80s and I think it's because when you're a kid, your sporting heroes really are a big deal to you.

Unashamedly, I do love the nostalgia of looking back at those days, particularly the evocative names of the grounds no longer with us such as The Boulevard, Watersheddings and of course Knowsley Road.

This book, however, is so much more than a walk through the 80s. This is the extraordinary story of a man born shortly before the Second World War who grew up to work in unimaginable conditions as a miner and who then joined the Mines Rescue Service to help his stricken colleagues after mining disasters. A man whose lifelong passion for rugby league burned so bright that he became a top referee then an assistant coach before becoming the longtime kitman to St Helens and Great Britain.

Stan has worked with all the top names in the sport of

rugby league for the past four decades and shares memories on the fun, friendships – and sometimes hardships – within that time period. Similarly, the contributors to this book read like a who's who of rugby league. If Stan has a tale on everyone in rugby league, then many of them have a tale on him in return. This book also provides a behind the scenes look at St Helens and international dressing rooms and lifts the lid on what you don't get to see.

The first time I met Stan was whilst I was editor of the St Helens fanzine *RUTT*. He arranged for me to give Sean Long our player of the season trophy whilst the players with the then coach Ellery Hanley were eating lunch in the Knowsley Road restaurant. I was somewhat in awe of Ellery so walked into the room shaking like a leaf but Stan's friendly, welcoming nature put me at ease.

I am old enough to remember him as a referee and apologise to him for all the things I may – or may not – have shouted at him when he was refereeing a Saints game. Sat as a kid on the paddock wall at Knowsley Road, I never would have dreamed I'd end up writing that very same referee's life story …

1

Fix Bayonets!

I was one of four boys, the third son my mum and dad had. There was Tom, Alf then me, then the youngest Harry. My early memories were connected with the war.

I was born in 1935 and I remember people having the Anderson air raid shelters that would be outside in your garden. They had run out of them though so we had to have an indoor shelter called a Morrison shelter, it was a table made of steel. It had four corner posts and a steel top. On the sides of it you could hang wire meshing. If there was an air raid, we would all get under the table then hang the wire meshing on the sides so if the house came in, we would be protected. The downside of that was anything you put on the top of the table was cold within minutes.

I lived in Atherleigh and a German plane came over us one night. The plane must have been on its way back to Germany and it dropped a couple of bombs on a nearby railway line. The next day, being kids, we had to go and have a look for ourselves. I found a piece of shrapnel, a fraction of the bomb.

Years later, when I was part of the backroom staff in the Great Britain Rugby League camp, after training and the evening meal there would be about ten backroom staff who would wind down over a cup of coffee with everybody telling stories. Phil Clarke, in particular, always loved the story of my eldest brother Tom joining the Home Guard –

and it really was a 'Dad's Army'. The first night when he came back, they had given him a steel helmet. We were all trying it on. The second time he went, they gave him another piece of equipment, this time it was a jacket. That went on until eventually he was fully clothed. We all had to try everything on. One night, Tom came home with a rifle and a bayonet. We were all very keen to have a go with that but fortunately there was no ammunition. In those daysour mother and father used to head off to the labour club on an evening. We couldn't wait for them to head out the door. Tom was stood to attention with his rifle showing us what to do. "Fix bayonets" went the cry as he did that. "Stance". Then facing the sofa, he said, "This is what you do. In. Twist. Out" going straight into the fabric with his bayonet. We all had to do it, our sofa was made of horsehair and it was all over the place.

After the rifle, Tom brought a Sten gun home with him. It was a short gun with a magazine on the side which could be used for rapid fire. I don't know where he'd got live ammunition from. My mum was pegging out washing in the back garden, Tom came to the back door and 'BANG-BANG-BANG' went the gun firing into the air. My mum passed out.

I also remember sleeping in an air raid shelter in Liverpool as we were due to be evacuated. They were planning to send us to Canada along with many other kids but in the end we didn't go as too many ships were being sunk. It wasn't frightening being in the air raid shelter. To me, as a kid, it was more of an adventure. I suppose I could have been living on the other side of the world now.

We'd play with wooden guns because of the war. My brother Alf once made a spear out of a brass stair rod. He had heated the end of it and flattened it with a hammer. We tried to use it to spear things in the water. He then started throwing it at my feet urging me to "dance". It landed on the floor and I set off running away. He picked it up, threw it at me and it went straight into the back of my leg. "Don't tell me mam," he begged.

He bought a second hand sword in a scabbard once from a shop. Our mum and dad had gone out so he said we should fence. Naturally, I got the scabbard whilst he had the sword. He stuck that in my hand as well. So, with one brother Tom with guns from the Home Guard and the other brother with spears and swords, it's a miracle I'm still here.

My other early memories involve our house and school. We lived in a council house on Wigan Road in Leigh. Back then with diseases such as scarlet fever, they used to come and fumigate your house. You would have to go outside your house whilst they did this. They would seal all your windows up and put a canister inside and you'd have to stay out of your house for so many hours before you were allowed to go back in.

I remember going into school eating 'lobby' or what some people call 'scouse'. Kids would be going to school in short pants back them. You didn't get a pair of long pants until you were much older.

At my infant's school, they didn't really play much sport. After that I went to Windermere Road Secondary Modern school. That was where rugby kicked in. With rugby, due to my small size, I would either play scrum half, winger or full back. I made it to the Lancashire side at schoolboy level.

I got caned at school every days as I was a bit of a yapper. You would get the cane on your hands then. There was Parsonage Colliery opposite my school where I would eventually work. When I was at school, a famous American boxer by the name of Joe Baksi came over to fight the British Champion, Bruce Woodcock. Boxing was a big thing when I was young and I remember sitting with my dad listening to fights on the radio. Baksi visited the colliery across the road from school and and my mates wanted to go and get Baksi's autograph in our dinner hour. We crossed the road, got his autograph and headed back over with big smiles on all of our faces but the headmaster Mr Parr was waiting for all of us with his cane behind his back.

"Have you seen the boxer?" he asked.

"Yeah", we replied.

"Have you all got his autograph?"

"Yeah".

"Well, I'm going to do a bit of boxing now. Two for the girls, four for the boys."

The girls got the cane once on each hand, the boys twice on each hand. Life was a bit different back then …

I wasn't a clever kid at school and have never been good at spelling. Thank God for the spellcheck on the computer today. We have friends in Africa and they used to tell me 'don't ever use spellcheck, we love the way you write in your emails'. I've come to the conclusion if you get the first and last letters of a word right, you can read it.

We used to come home from school, change our clothes, get into some old things and get out onto the field and start playing with a ball. We were into bird nesting a lot then. We collected bird's eggs – something that's rightly frowned upon these days. There were two large expanses of water near where I lived, one which had sunk and had become a farm. We would take our pants off and wade out into the water and look for frogs and newts.

Me and Billy Costello, a friend of mine who lived in the same street as me, went across to an old colliery one day where the mine had shut. The shaft went down hundreds of feet and they'd put a seal on it about 30 feet down. This particular shaft had become overgrown with shrubs and Billy fell down it. I was terrified because I couldn't see or hear him and thought he had been killed so I ran home to get help. Our dads returned to the shaft with the Police and they had to climb down on ropes. Fortunately Billy was alive although he had broken his arm. He was very lucky indeed.

They were hard times after the war. As soon as you got home from school, you would be told to take your school clothes off and put your old clothes on. We would be out playing in the street most of the time, throwing a rag ball around. On a Sunday, my Dad my eldest brother would go the club and gamble on 'pitch and toss'. They would have a skinful of ale and then go and play 'piggy' on the field. As the youngest, I would stand guard and look out for the police coming as gambling was illegal then. I'm sure the coppers knew what was going on and turned a bit of a blind eye to it as it wasn't really bad.

I loved watching rugbyand we had some great players at Leigh. When I was a young lad, there was Trevor Allan, one of my favourite players, and the first Australian we had. He had a skull cap and was a tackling machine. He got a house near the Greyhound hotel at Leigh. When he arrived in the town, he couldn't get over the smog. There was lots of heavy industry and everybody had a coal fire back then so air pollution was a big issue. The other guy who came was Rex Mossop. He made a big name for himself. I remember at the time thinking he was a giant but looking back at the programmes he was only fourteen and a half stone. I bet James Roby weighs more than him now and he's not one of our bigger players at Saints. Rugby players then didn't do weightlifting. The muscles that they had came from the industries they worked in. A lot of players worked in the pit such as the Wigan player Ted Slevin. He was a giant of a bloke but his muscles were from manual work.

Those players at Leigh were idols back then. Mossop signed for Leigh for the huge sum of £4,000 and Piet Botha, the full back from South Africa who was an excellent goalkicker, also joined the club. Saints got Vollenhoven from South Africa of course. So, the game did have an influx of overseas players back then. Players would get £10 for a win, £8 for a draw and £6 for a defeat. Leigh also had the sprint champion McDonald Bailey. He only played one game, scoring one try. He was absolutely petrified.

After school, I needed to get a job. I had loved woodwork

at school and made some nice pieces. I was quite good with my hands and made a wooden fruit bowl and a three tier cake stand. However, I couldn't get a job in joinery. To add insult to injury, I had a mate who was crap at joinery yet he got a job in it.

My dad was a miner as was my eldest brother. They didn't want me working down the pitas they knew it was dangerous, dirty and dusty work. So I went to work in the cotton industry at the Tunnicliffe Factory. However I only lasted six weeks at the mill, talk about being hot, it was like an oven. They were using spinning mules to stretch the raw cottonand they had to have it at a certain heat. I just worked in a brace and bib, no shirt, nothing on my feet on the wooden floors. They had me sweeping cotton up and I knew I didn't want to stay there long so I packed it in to go to work at the foundry.

Working at the foundry was a very skilful job making moulds. You would have black sand and mix it with water to make it damp. If you were making an iron wheel, you would be given a pattern wooden wheel. You would put the pattern in the sand and pat it, like you would a child's sandcastle. When you took the pattern off, it left the shape of one side of the wheel in the sand. You'd do the other half of the wheel in another steel box full of sand. Then you would carefully turn one of the boxes over and place it on the first one to make the mould for the complete wheel. In the afternoon, the iron would be melted and poured into the box. The art of it was if any of the sand fell out, it would obviously make a difference to the shape. I was given a range of tools I had never seen in my life before to stick the bits of sand backin.

In the morning, it would be freezing because it had to be cold when you were working with the moulds. In the afternoon, it would be roasting because they would be melting the iron. Then there would be the molten metal coming out of the furnaces.

Working with the sand would leave me as dirty as any miner. There were no showers back then so every day I would go home and have a bath. The foundry was as dirty as mining, it was filthy. The pay was only £2 per week. All my mates were working in the mines and were bragging that they got £5 a week so reluctantly my dad let me go into mining.

2

At the Coalface

Seams of coal run at different depths in our country. In Lancashire, the depths of the better seams of coal are deep. In years gone by in the Wigan and Leigh area, you would take the sod off the top of the ground, take a bit of clay out then you'd come to a seam of coal which was near the surface. All early miners did with those seams was dig down into a pit, hack the coal out with a spade and bring it up in a bucket on a pulley. They'd dig as far as they could to get the coal out using that system. Once they got too deep, there would be a lack of ventilation. They'd go a hundred yards further across then dig down again, those were called Bell pits because the hole in the ground was the shape of a bell. That was the system that had always been used.

I have a map of Bell pits all over the Wigan area that never got filled in properly. When a pit closes now, they go so far down, put a bridge across and then they fill it in from the top.

With coal that is close to the surface, the mining companies operate what is called a drift mine. If the seam was say, a hundred metres deep they would dig a tunnel and go down on a slope until they got to the seam. They then work that seam like the cream in a cream cake using a conveyor belt to get the coal away. With deeper seams, such as those eight hundred metres down, they would put a shaft in.

There was one in Bolton that was called Brackley Colliery.

They worked that seam out as a drift mine. When it was finished, they bricked it up at the top to stop people going in. Over years, this brickwork deteriorated. Once in the late 1960s there was a gang of kids missing. Other children who knew the missing kids said that they had made a den in the colliery tunnel. The fire brigade went to Brackley and found a hole in the wall. These kids had gone through this hole. A fireman went in after them and never came back out. They sent for Mines Rescue who attended with breathing apparatus. When they went down there they found three dead kids and a dead fireman. With the slope of the mine, the poisonous gasses which often form underground, many of which are heavier than air, had settled at the bottom. When the kids went down into the mine the gasses had killed them. So, a team was put together to go up and down the country locating tunnels where mines and the small bell pits had been to try and prevent further tragedies.

Over in Yorkshire, their seams of coal were closer to the surface and were bigger seams. However, the best quality coal was in deep seams, eight hundred metres down such as at Bold Colliery in St Helens. That's why it was so expensive to mine coal in this country.

I started life as a miner as Bickershaw Colliery. I remember a little funny experience when I first started down the pit. My Dad was always on afternoon turn while I was on morning turn. Morning turn was six in the morning till two in the afternoon. Afternoon turn was two in the afternoon till ten at night. The miners would travel up and down the mine in what were called cages. As I was finishing my turn and was getting out of the cage, the afternoon turn were queuing up to go into it. I saw my Dad in this queue and shouted 'Hi Dad'. Everybody turned round. I was that black nobody knew who's son I was. After that, I would always call him by his first name Ernie when at the pit. There would be between six and seven hundred men waiting to go down in that queue.

It could be physical, dirty work but it was a way of life. The characters in mining were unbelievable and the camaraderie was excellent. I did six months at Bickershaw then I moved to Parsonage because my mates were there. It was only down the road and you could swap pits then. Parsonage was the deepest mine in England at the time, it was over a thousand yards deep. You could walk for miles underground, from Leigh towards Warrington. You could come home in their time, so if your shift was finishing at 2pm you could start travelling underground around 1.30pm. In the morning, you had to travel in your own time. I was getting up at 5.00am every day.

If you can think of an army, you have your front line fighting. All those at the front have to be supplied by those at the back. They cannot fight on the front line without munitions and food. It's the same thing with mining. You had your coalface which would only be a metre high. Your first job as a young man in the pit was getting supplies to the front line – the coalface. This was called haulage work. I would take supplies on wooden carts on rails to the coalface. I would be taking things like supports for the roof, a lot of it was wood in my early days. The distance to the coalface was so far that I would take it halfway then others would take it the rest of the way. I did a couple of years haulage work. That was the lower paid end of mining. The money was on the front line, so naturally everybody wanted to get onto the coalface. I eventually ended up working on the coalface when I was around 20-years-old then I would be on my hands and knees for eight hours a day in a seam that was no more than three feet high. The roof of the seam was all like cockleshells, you could see where the sea had been millions of years ago. I got quite a few fossils, not in the coal but in the rock, the separation.

If you think of the strata which is underground, from the top you've got grass, you dig down and you've got soil then clay, and you eventually come to rock. In the Leigh area, the coal was very deep underground. I would be working at around 900 yards deep which was one of the deepest pits in Britain. Layers of coal come in different thicknesses which would be given different names. There was Peacock, Trencherbone and Black and White. The Peacock seam was about a three feet high. That coalface stretched for about two hundred yards. To work the coal out they had a man every five yards. In the afternoon would be the bloody hard job of drilling, putting holes along the width of the seam. A couple of guys would then come in with explosives and fill the holes with them; that's the job my Dad used to do. He was helping the deputiesand once they'd charged so many they'd get out of the way and fire the charges. When we got there in a morning, we would have to shift a big pile big pile of debris from the blasting. We would get on our knees and dig but as we moved forward, we had to support the roof because we were going into virgin ground. It was tough, dirty and bloody hard work. Behind us was a to put the coal on. If some of it hadn't blown up properly we had picks to break it down. I worked on the coalface for most of my time down there.

At the weekend the rugby was the main thing since there was no telly. I only bought my first telly when I got married. A lot of mines had closed in Wigan so their miners came to work in Leigh. The rivalry underground with Wigan and Leigh was incredible although it was all good banter. There was a lot of rivalry between Wigan and Leigh, especially when it came time for the derby game, but it was all in good sport. They never came to blows down the pit. With Wigan miners coming down into Leigh pits, even though they were so close to us in terms of miles, the lingo was a lot different. They would say 'kicked a goal through the postses'; they'd never say 'posts'. Family still pick me up on the way that I talk but your dialect is steeped into you. Some people say you should keep your dialect. One fella once said to me what sounded like, "I've just decorated tharse and I can't see a giant" but what was really "I've just decorated my house and I can't see the joint between the paper".

The lifestyle of miners was pie and a pint, work hard, play hard. Monday morning, you would get in that cage going down and it would hold about forty miners. They would all have been on the ale all weekend and many of them would be breaking wind. Usually some wag would say, "If you don't like it, bleeding get out" as you were heading down into the earth.

People don't realise you had no facilities underground, you had to carry your own can of water and your own sandwiches every day. Water was liquid gold in the mine, no exaggeration; you looked after that like nothing else. Because of the system of ventilating a mine, a fan would suck it through one shaft, all through the workings and then up the other shaft. By the time the air got to where we were working, the temperature around us was about 90 degrees Fahrenheit. Originally we would carry water in an aluminium can, then they banned aluminium because it can create a hot spark which could cause a gas explosion. We would be given a twenty minute break to eat our sandwiches; some lads would eat their sandwiches then sleep for the rest of the break. Sometimes we would have to work through the break.

We were overrun with mice down the mine which meant we had to protect our food. We would use detonator wire which we tied around our sandwiches and hang them up. If you didn't do that, the mice get at them. If you used string, the mice could climb down it but they couldn't cling on to the wire. I learnt that lesson on my first day when I tied mine up using a piece of string. I got to my sandwiches and knew the mice had been at them "Shit!" It was dark but I could see the hole in the four sandwiches where a mouse had just eaten its way through my lunch. That day was a case of asking my mate for a butty.

I used to put celery in my water down the pit as it used

to give it a slight taste. It was all about anything moist down the pit as water was your life. You'd put jam on a slice of cheese and that would be quite nice. Any meat underground wouldn't be nice as it would go dry. After the war, foreigners brought over things like salami which we got into. We had a lot of Ukrainians come over who were great workers and great people. The Poles brought in their style of food.

I started off at a fiver a week down the pit and even when they said we were getting good money, it was only up to thirty quid a week when I was working my heart out on the coalface. Times have changed.

People used to keep ferrets back then and would use them for catching rabbits. One of the lads down the pit called Dino Casilli was really into ferreting and would go out in the middle of the night. We were paid weekly down the mine and Friday was payday. On the night shift in the colliery, the people who were coming off it would be coming off at six o clock in the morning. They'd get a shower and then go and collect their wages. It was a paydesk just like you'd get in a post office. You'd give your number in and they'd give you your wage packet. Dino had been out ferreting and came into the paydesk with a double barrelled shotgun wearing a balaclava as he had been out in the early hours of the morning. He frightened the pay staff to death. He'd never given it a thought.

There were all sorts of comical incidents like that such as two of the guys who worked on one of the coalface machines. One day one of them said "Bloody television, the wife wants to move it into the back room but I'm not going on the roof to run a new cable from the aerial."

The other said, "You don't need go on your roof, go outside, grab your cable, walk away, it will pull all the clips out of the wall, get a brick, tie it to the end of the cable and throw it over the roof".

"I never thought of that".

The day after, the following conversation took place.

"Now, how'd you get on?"

"Just the job, I didn't need to drill a hole for it come back in, it came over and went straight through the back window".

Another day, someone's telly wasn't working and he was told it was probably the fuse in his telly. He was told to get a packet of fags which all had silver paper in then, get a bit of the silver paper and put it in the fuse. The day after he came with a burnt hand. He had put the silver paper in and blown up the television! There were stories like this in abundance.

There would be a lot of arguing at times down the pit and a lot of swearing – effing and blinding – it was second nature. There would be some fall outs. There were two men in particular who were real rivals. One day, a section of the coalface collapsed and it hit one of these men and it snapped his leg, breaking his tibia and fibia. His rival was one of the first to get to him and give him a lift by digging him out. They got him on a stretcher and the first thing he said to him was, "Bill, you'll not need your butties now will you? I'll have them". No compassion.

3

Getting in Bother

Down the pit we did have one piece of equipment we could travel in and it was called a man riding gang. Almost like a cable car, it was a rope that pulled it along. We were waiting one day for the carriage to come in to take us out. The afternoon turn would be coming out on it and then the next turn would come in on it. It came in this day and it hadn't quite stopped when I jumped on it. I looked next to me to see the deputy manager Corfield sat there. He asked me how I had got on the carriage. I told him it had nearly stopped when I got on and he asked me what would have happened if I had broken my leg, before going onto say I would have claimed off them. He said when I had finished my shift I should go up to his office. I worked that day, had my wash and went up to his office. He asked me how much money per day I got at the pit. I told him it was two pound fifty and he said, "You're worked for nothing today". He stopped me that day's wages.

On the Friday evening of that same week I was playing rugby for the pit. We were playing at Leigh Miners. I sprung my shoulder during the game. I had to come off and go to hospital. One of the bosses said he would get somebody to run me to the hospital which was about two miles away. Lo and behold, it was Corfield who came to take me. I said I didn't want him to take me to the hospital as he had stopped me a days pay and that I would walk it before letting him take me. He couldn't do anything to me then as I was in my own time. He said, "Let me tell you something, when I'm down the pit I have a job to do. I've to do it to the laws of the mine. What I did was to the laws of the mine. Get in my car, I'm taking you to the hospital".

I was high spirited as a young lad, a bit like Sean Long many years later. They had Magneto phones down the pit about every 250 metres. One was ringing so I picked it up, I was asked who I was and gave him my name. He asked where I was speaking from and I replied, "Radio Luxembourg, where are you speaking from?"

"Manager's office, call in when you come up".

It was on my mind all day and after I had got washed I headed up there. I gave my name to the secretary, she told me to sit down. I waited an hour; this was after eight hours hard work. He brought me in.

"Oh this is the man from Radio Luxembourg isn't it".

"It was just a bit of fun".

"Working down a mine's not fun. It's serious. Next time you're on the phone and somebody speaks to you, I want you to reply to them properly. I'll let you off this time".

He hadn't really let me off though as he had made me waste an hour of my own time.

Under the ground, methane was a big problem. Wherever there's coal there's methane gas. There's other gases as well underground. Methane would only explode at a certain percentage. When it gets to about five per cent it would start to explode with a spark or flame. More with six percent upwards until you went over fifteen per cent and it wouldn't explode. It would be too rich. That's why we had to teach the officials who ran the collieries. We had deputies who took the oil lamps for testing for gas. If it was one percent, you couldn't see a change in the flame on the lamp but at one and a half percent the flame would alter slightly, and there would be a tiny blue haze on top of it. At three percent, this would be a perfect blue haze triangle. They'd go round with these lamps testing. There's certain parts of a mine you are liable to get gases more than others. If they found a dangerous percentage of gas then something had to be done about it. They'd have to switch machinery off and things of that nature. Eventually, we used to drill holes in the strata. That's the argument they're having today about shale gas. They drill into the strata, hit the gas, put pipes in then pump it off.

I have always watched rugby from being a kid. I was an avid Leigh fan, as was my now wife Celia. She used to go to the games with her sister before we started courting. The match was everything back then. When the Australians came over to tour, they would play a number of league teams as well as the tests. One tour I was on shift work at the pit; I was on the afternoon shift which clashed with the Aussies playing at Leigh. It was a lovely day, my mate came round and we were sat in a field talking about that night's momentous game. One of us said, "Shall we go?"

"We'll lose a big whack of money if we don't go to work."

"They only come once every four years."

"Look at this weather, gorgeous isn't it?"

"We'll waste a day of our life if we go into the pit."

The decision was made, we were going to the game. Those are the special days I do remember.

In December and January, supporters would go to the ground to set braziers up on the field to clear the ice so the game could go ahead. All through the night, we would be putting coke on the braziers to keep them burning. The match was the be all and end all. There wouldn't be any groundsheets then so we'd put straw on the pitch the night before a match then cart it all off before kick off.

I worked with a lad down the pit called Kenny Ashcroft who had a bit of a smallholding. He had a Jack Russell which had had two pups. He gave one of the pups to his brother. Now on a Sunday then, people would always go to their mum's for tea. Kenny's brother brought his young pup with him to his mum's. It was jumping all over the furniture and barking. Kenny's dad said, "Shut that bloody dog up and get it trained. Look at its mother there Bess."

Bess was sat quietly, and while the dad was eating a plate of liver and onions, he said, "I could put this plate in front of her and she wouldn't touch it". His son disagreed so he put the plate down in front of the dog and told her to stay. The dog did as she was told and he said, "That's how you should train your dog". The son told him that if he moved away it would eat the food. The dad vehemently disagreed and walked out into the kitchen. Kenny chipped in now with, "Go on Bess, get it eaten," and the dog cleared the lot. The dad returned and said, "I don't know how that's happened".

They kept hens and chickens on that smallholding too. There comes a time when hens stop laying eggs. Kenny would say to us we could have them for a few shillings for cooking into chicken broth. On one Friday afternoon we went down the pit at two o clock, coming back up at ten o clock. Before we'd even got changed, Kenny headed over to his car, opened up his boot and there were about a dozen hens there, still alive. "One for you Stan," he said and wrung its neck. On the Monday he asked me how it was and I told him it was fine and it had had a couple of yolks in it. He explained that they wouldn't have fully formed but that would be an extra shilling as I could have made custard with them!

It was all big families then. I remember a bloke working with me who had 22 kids and I had a good mate, Tommy, at the pit who had eight kids. I always tell this story to Phil Clarke and Brian Carney as they love tales about mining. Brian, in particular, wouldn't leave me alone every time I was on tour, wanting to hear all the tales from down the pit. So, anyway my mate with the eight kids, him and his wife never got to go out together. It was club life, he would go down to the club. He was a pit man but when he dressed up, he was as smart as anybody you had ever seen. He looked like Clark Gable with his pencil moustache, lovely wavy hair and a beautiful suit. One night a week, his wife would go to the bingo at the club whilst he looked after the kids. In them days it wasn't disposable nappies, you had to wash them and hang them on the line. They would sell nappies and soaps at the pit canteen and miners would get them a little bit cheaper. It was a little perk for us. So, this night she went to the bingo, I saw Tommy down the pit the next day and asked him how he had got on.

"What a night I had with that lot," he said. "They were crying, falling out, I was changing shitty nappies. There was three of them running around without a nappy on. I thought I'm not sticking this any longer. I brought the tin bath in and filled it up with buckets of hot water. It was like a bloody sheep dip, I dunked them in one by one and then threw each of them to bed. I got them all in bed but one of them kept crying. I was losing it so I went up and shouted, 'If you don't shut up I'm going to smack your arse'. He said, 'Mister, I don't live here.'"

He'd only bathed somebody else's kid. Kids used to play in one another's houses all the time back then. It was council estates and your neighbours were your best friends. On the nicer nights, everybody would be at their front gate chatting because they had nothing to do. That was the way of life.

Tommy taught me how to decorate, since he had to decorate his own house every three months with so many kids. He showed me how to hang paper. Unfortunately he came to a tragic end while he was decorating his stairs. They had a wooden hand rail, and you could unscrew this hand rail and take it off so that he could drop the wallpaper behind it. There were brackets that came out of the wall to hold the rail. He was carrying one of the kids and fell from the top of the stairs. In protecting his child, he hit his head on one of the brackets and it killed him. He had gone through all the dangers of the pit and it was something so unassuming that had killed him. We had gone through some horrendous times me and him.

I played rugby at this time too, I played scrum half, hooker, winger and full back. After playing on a lot of very bad pitches, there would be no shower facilities so I would go home and my Dad would always run me a bath, putting Radox in. It was really nice to soak in it. Looking back, I shouldn't have been doing that because if you have any bruises, hot water makes them bleed more. Cold water is far better, it's just not as pleasant to lie in. My mum, Doris, would be saying I was too small to play rugby and my dad would tell her to leave me alone. My dad was very strict about my rugby gear, as soon as I got home I would be told to take my boots off, stuff paper in them to keep the shape of the boot, brush the loose mud off them, and then the next day when they had dried a bit they would be given the wire brush treatment. After that, they would be polished.

There wasn't much to do back then so rugby was the be all and end all of your life. If you were into it, that is. I was one of four lads and was the only one who played rugby.

4

Celia

I started courting at 17 through the dance halls which was our leisure back then. Young people were into dancing to the music of the big bands. I loved jiving and jitterbugging. Going back to the war days, we had the Burtonwood air base close by, and all the big band music came over with the Americans. I remember getting on my bike to go to Burtonwood as a lad watching the planes come in.

It was on a Saturday night out dancing that I met Celia. It was a temperance bar so there was no alcohol. You'd have a glass of Vimto or dandelion and burdock. Celia came from a rugby family, her uncle Joe Cartwright played for Leigh and England and went to Australia. It was good that she came from such a background because when we did start courting, we had something in common straightaway.

Celia came from Atherton. Her dad and brother were both miners. Her dad had said to her, "I don't care who you go out with so long as it's not a miner". I was terrified of going their house. He said, "I know what they're like them lads because I work with them". They were no different from any other lads though, he just knew mining lads. Celia would always come to Leigh on a Saturday night as it was a bit bigger place than Atherton. I'd put her on a bus back to the centre of Atherton at the end of the night. There was the odd time that I would go to Atherton and walk it back to Leigh.

I was playing amateur rugby at the time for a team called Wigan Road Juniors. Our under 21s side was a good team and we once went a full season without losing a match. Micky Martyn, the uncle of former Oldham and Saints player Tommy, played for us. He was an outstanding player who went on to play for Leigh and Great Britain.

We played on some crap fields at the time and there was even a pitch referred to as Iodine Park as you needed the stuff on you after playing on there. On one occasion I had cut my knees and I was murder for my cuts getting septic. My knees were all swollen up so my mum had put on a kaolin poultice. I'll never forget, my mate came round as I took the bandage off. You had to squeeze the wound a bit to get the puss out but this time it burst and blood and puss went everywhere. My mate passed out. During this period of having the bad knee, I was supposed to be seeing Celia. I spoke to my sister-in-law and she said she would see Celia and tell her that I couldn't get out. My mum must have overheard me because she said, "What's all this about a girlfriend?" I told her about Celia and she asked me where she lived. She then told my sister-in-law Veronica, "If she wants, she can come and see him". Celia was the youngest of eight kids, as people all had big families then. She was quite apprehensive about coming to our house.

Celia enjoys telling the story now as she says that I looked well. We had no carpets in our house, it was all lino and I was sat in an old rocking chair by a coal fireplace. My mother had put a shawl around me too. Celia couldn't believe that this 19-year-old lad had a shawl round him and didn't know what she was coming to.

Back then, 21 seemed to the golden age for getting married. We'd courted two-and-a-half years by the time I turned 21 and we got married on the 10th March 1956. Brian Chadwick, one of my mates and an outstanding rugby player as a young lad, was getting married the same day. He was getting married in the morning and told me he wanted me to be groomsman. I told him I was getting married that afternoon but I still did it for him. We then went to Waterfields restaurant for our lunch.

In the afternoon, Brian and his new bride Kathleen came to our wedding at three o clock. We got married at Atherton church. The reception was in a pub across the way. The four of us left the pub at 10 o clock at night and we got a taxi from Atherton to Bolton, we then got a bus to Blackpool.

We had five days at Blackpool. We had a cracking time. We got back from Blackpool on the Monday and we were then living with Celia's mum and dad. From leaving school, I had never kept any of my wages; I had always given them to my mum. She would tell me that if I worked any overtime I could keep that for myself so I tried to work as much overtime as I could. The week before I got married I gave her my wage packet but she gave it me back.

I told Celia I had work on Monday and asked her what we had for 'jackbit' (that was the word for sandwiches). She got her purse out, gave me half a crown and told me to get something off the tea trolley.

"Tea trolley down a pit?" I said gobsmacked. "Where do you think I work?"

In the July, we went to the Isle of Man for a holiday. We flew over and stayed in a boarding house. The landlady showed us to our room. We had hardly put our bags out before the landlady came back to the room. She told us that she had just had a phone call from the person who had stayed in the room prior to us saying she had left a bag with some money in under the mattress. The landlady then lifted every corner of the mattress but there was no bag there. She apologised for disturbing us and went to phone the woman back. I turned the mattress over completely and right in the middle was the bag. I opened it and was knocked back as there must have been £500 in it in old, dirty notes. I had never seen so much money especially when you think I was only earning about £2 a day. My first house only cost £1,500.

My head was going ninety to the dozen with what to do with this money; it could be a deposit for a house for us. Celia was adamant that we hand it in. I was like Del Boy, "Whoa, let's not do anything rash, let's sit down and have a think about this". I thought that the past guest in the room must have been a prostitute. I felt we could either hide the money or I could get my brother to come over and take it home for us. Celia insisted she wouldn't be able to sleep if we took the money. She won in the end of course and I handed the bag in to the landlady.

The landlady thanked me but she never came back later to tell me the woman had been back for her bag. Who's to say the landlady didn't keep it? I didn't even get a reward.

Just before another holiday, I suffered a bad injury; I'd had my nose broken three times back then, twice playing rugby and once playing cricket. We always had knockout competitions at the pit. We didn't play football but would play rugby and also cricket. We'd have us miners plus teams of electricians calling themselves 'bright sparks' competing against each other. The mechanics would be the 'oily rags'. We had an eight-team knockout competition. We played a cricket match on the Friday night and on the Monday morning I was going to Spain for the very first time. I was batting and it came to the last ball of the over. The ball came off the shoulder of the bat and hit me straight on the nose. It put me down to the floor and when I got up I was in a right mess. My eyes had come up in no time at all and my nose was bleeding. I went off to hospital. As well as the nurses, they had nuns there who were learning to stitch. They stitched up my nose and my eyes were by now out like puddings. The doctor came in and told me that they couldn't do anything at that particular time to reset my nose. He continued that they needed to let it heal a bit. He told me that I would have to come back in three or four days. I told him I couldn't due to going to Spain. He told me if I didn't come back he wouldn't be able to reset my nose and if I left it two weeks it would set itself. I told him it would have to stay that way as this was the third time I'd had my nose broken but I had never been to Spain.

I came home that night from the hospital and Celia said, "We're not going abroad". My eyes were virtually closed. I told her that it was only swelling and that it would go down. So, I didn't go back to hospital and I did go to Spain. The Spanish would be doing boxing gestures towards me asking, "You boxer?" I just went along with that. There was no way I could explain what cricket was to them. I came back after the two weeks and one of my eyes was ok but the other was still part shut. It gradually sorted itself out.

5

Picking up the Whistle

I played rugby league until I was 25 whilst working down the pit at the same time. I had a couple of little injuries that had caused me to have time off work which we really couldn't afford due to having young children by then. Celia and I had moved into our own house at 22. I would train a couple of nights a week and play on some awful pitches at the weekend. I never got any major injuries playing rugby, just cuts, bumps and bruises.

The roof of the mine collapsed once whilst I was down the pit, it knocked a steel support out which hit my foot and broke it. I was off work then for five weeks and couldn't play rugby. Celia said, "Do you not think you should pack the rugby in? I'll not stop you but we can't afford for you to be off work getting injured playing rugby".

As soon as I finished playing, a bloke by the name of Harry Hunt came to me. He had been a referee and had refereed the famous Wembley final between Wigan and St Helens when Alex Murphy had kicked Wigan to death. He lived locally and told me that he wanted me to start refereeing. I couldn't be bothered doing it to be honest; it was one thing playing but refereeing didn't appeal to me at that time. He told me they were struggling for amateur referees but I told him I didn't want to do it.

He got in touch with me one day saying there was a match at Leigh and they had no referee. I told him I wouldn't know what to do but he advised me to referee it like I thought I should, like I would as a player. He asked me to do it as a favour to him. I went down and I was probably dreadful as I had never read the rulebook. That's how I kicked into refereeing though. I went on refereeing amateurs for ages. My dad kept on asking me why didn't I go and do my refereeing exam. I told him I didn't think I was clever enough for that. He insisted I should have a go. I had joined the referee's society in Leigh, got a rulebook and had begun to swot up on it.

They would do the exam twice a year, once in Manchester and once in Yorkshire. I went to the Manchester one and failed it. The hardest questions were on refereeing signals. I knew them but I didn't know how to get them down on paper. Think about it, all rugby league fans know the gesture for a knock-on but how many could describe that gesture in writing? It always sticks in my mind, the letter of the law, "with palms of the hands facing outwards, fingertips pointing to the ground, make two or three pushing movements below the knee in a forward direction". There were twenty five questions like that. I had an hour to do the exam and I didn't finish it. There were people who jumped up out of the room after forty five minutes who were teachers like Gerry Kershaw and Sam Shepherd; they knew how to do exams. We had a few teachers as referees then. Seeing them get up having finished with time to spare made me worse. I was a pit man, I wasn't a teacher. My dad told me not to worry and to try again, so six months down the line I tried again. That time, I passed it.

I started refereeing late at 25 as they often start refereeing now at 11-years-old. The system has all changed.

When I passed my exam, I ran the line as a touch judge at Colts and A team matches. I then progressed to refereeing Colts matches. I was 38-years-old before I got into first team refereeing. I was always fit though and could run a bit too. The positions I had played in the game meant I was pretty nippy. I'm not saying I was as fast as Jonny Lomax but I was pretty quick. I was just on the stepping stone of getting one or two first team matches by this point.

Refereeing amateur rugby had given me a good grounding because the games were tough, especially at places like Pilkington Recs and Leigh Miners. They would always be physical, hard games. I think the referees today are not getting that apprenticeship. You'd get all the old pros going back into the amateur game and they knew all the tricks of the trade – and they would use them! I progressed by running the line as a touch judge for Colts rugby. Then I started refereeing Colts rugby and being touch judge at A team games and so the progression continued. I eventually became a grade two referee which meant I could referee first team and A team games. A grade one referee would only do first team games.

6

Cronton Mining Disaster

During this period, I had joined the Mines Rescue Service at work. For every hundred men you had you had to have one member of the Mines Rescue. Our local main station wasBoothstown which was just like a fire station. They had 15 or 20 full-time rescuers there who lived in a row of houses by the side of the station. They were on call all the time. If anything happened at the collieries they would jump in the van, and whilst this was happening the superintendent at the station would get in touch with Bickershaw and Parsonage Collieries to get part-timers like me. Whatever we were doing we would have to stop and come up the pit and get across to the colliery where the incident was.

As part of the Mines Rescue Service, you had to have a strict medical and exercise test every year. You would wear a harness during this which would be the same weight as your rescue set. There would be a box in front of you which you would have to step on and off to a metronome. You would do this over a five-minute period.

In my time doing mines rescue, there were two big episodes. One was at Cronton where there were three lives lost and the other was at Golborne where 11 died.

Cronton, in particular, sticks in my mind. It was the 21st of August, 1972. Saturday night going into Sunday morning when we got a knock on the front door at four o clock as we didn't have a phone then. I answered the door to a policeman who told me I was wanted at Cronton Colliery straightaway for mines rescue. I put my clothes on wondering what I would be going to. You had no idea what scene would await when you got there.

He took me in the police car as I didn't have transport at the time. I got there to be told that there had been an explosion and that there were two men missing. The first thing you had to do in such incidents was to go and see the doctor on site who would give you a quick check over. My heart was racing, but that's normal in an adrenalin fuelled situation like that. This night there were two pit men who couldn't go down as they had been to the pub. Another lad had been sunburned on his back so he wasn't allowed down either. They wouldn't let you down as part of the rescue if you'd been drinking because you became a liability once down there. The lad who had a sunburned back couldn't go down because the heavy pack would just rub his back to pieces. Each rescue worker wore rescue apparatus that weighed 48 pounds which made you become half the man in terms of your moving speed.

As it was weekend, they only had an inspection team on, a deputy and electrician who were carrying out safety inspections. After a team briefing we split up into teams of five and descended underground.

In the meantime, the Boothstown full-time brigade had already gone in ahead and set up a fresh air base. This was done by travelling in slowly with one member carrying a canary and keeping an eye on it. A canary is used because its heart rate is fifteen times faster than a human so it detects the carbon monoxide quicker than a person can and would fall off its perch (carbon monoxide is always present after a fire or explosion) this determined the fresh air base because you cannot travel in any further without putting on your face mask and switching on your oxygen.

As we arrived at this point we were told to stay there as a team was on its way out. They had discovered one body and brought it out. Another team went in and brought out a second.

The only form of communication when wearing the oxygen mask was a small horn attached to our apparatus. We had a series of signals like one for stop, two for forward and three for retreat.

Once the bodies had been recovered, there was no need to look for anything else. They then had to re-establish that 'warzone' if you like. They needed to know what had caused it and why. They also needed to rid the area of all the foul air.

The two bodies were naked; the blast had completely shredded their clothes.

A team of men went back in to assess the situation in order that we could determine how we would tackle it. Our oxygen sets only lasted two hours and given it took half-an-hour from the fresh air base to get in and the same to get back, that meant we only had a maximum working time of an hour at the incident

I went in and there was bent metal and shattered rocks. All the thick electrical cables were twisted. We grafted for an hour then the next team took over until we got the fan established to blow out all the foul air. It took four days all in all to clear.

The investigators reckoned there had been a rock fall. There had been a ventilation fan in, and the rock fall had brought some of the electrical cable down, cutting through it in the process. The fan had gone off as a result of that so they had brought the electrician down to see why the fan had gone off. They had an electrical box down there and the trip switch had gone down in the box once the fan had gone off. The electrician had told his apprentice to go back to the transformer and reset it. He did this and the cable must have sparked where it had fractured. And because the fan had been off, gas had accumulated and up it went. They were all killed with the blast so severe that metal fencing was found inside their bodies.

With working in mines rescue, you never thought of the danger until after you'd done the rescue. We would work in appalling conditions.

There was also an explosion at Golborne Colliery where eleven people died, including two of my good friends who I'd worked with at Parsonage Colliery. They were on contract work and they got paid for what they did. Contract workers would be separate teams of men doing different jobs. These two of my friends had moved to Golborne doing contract work. When the explosion had taken place, the men who hadn't been hit by the direct impact of the blast had been killed by the hot gasses which had scorched down the tunnel, burning them inside their lungs as well as on the outside of their bodies. Two of the men who died were the Grainey brothers, who were attached to Leigh Miners and there's a trophy with their name on to this day as an end of season competition.

In the case of a fire or explosion miners were issued with a small device called a self rescuer which was a mini respirator intended to give them time to evacuate the tunnel when the air had become toxic. They carried this on their belts.

It was such a hard industry. The pressure of the strata would buckle girders. The tunnels didn't keep nice and straight. I remember we went through a period where every day the roof would cave in. I suffered broken toes through this. It would be hard to carry a man out on a stretcher underground in ninety degree heat over the three mile distance from the coalface to the shaft. You had to have at least eight men to carry one. Four would carry him for a while then swap over with the other four. There was very little underground transport in the early days.

I had a first aid certificate down the mine which qualified me to give morphine. Every two hundred and fifty yards they would have a little safe which would hold two ampoules of morphine. First aiders would have a morphine key. It was like a little toothpaste tube with a needle on the end, you'd find a vein, stick it in and squeeze the morphine through. I saw a few really bad injuries down there. One mechanic was lifting a piece of machinery, which came down on his hand. We had to lift the machinery off him and his fingers were like pennies. He lost two and a half fingers. Joey was the lad's name and he ended up coming back to work.

One roof collapse saw a man break his tibia and fibia with the bones sticking out through his leg. That was a bad one. It was a bit sickening.

It got to the stage where I would come home at night thinking of the dangers of working underground and it meant I wasn't sleeping well at all. I finished up grinding my teeth a lot with the stress of it. I'd be asleep then jump in bed wakening myself up. It was starting to keep Celia awake it got that bad. I went to my doctor and they made me a gumshield, to stop me grinding my teeth together.

I'd finish my mining shift at two in the afternoon and go in the shower area at the pit, where there'd be two hundred men showering all facing each other in big lines. We'd be washing, laughing and joking. The loofah's we had back then were the proper ones from under the sea. You'd always say to the man facing you in the shower, "Wash me back pal," and you'd turn so he could wash your back then vice versa. If your loofah was brand new, it would nearly rub the skin off you. That's such a contrast to the rugby league dressing room now where some of the younger players will wear Speedos in the shower. I think that's because they've never had jobs and have always just lived with their families.

Back then I would be getting home about half past two in the afternoon. Celia was working at the time and would finish at five o clock. I would always go home tired after a shift on my hands and knees with a spade digging coal. The first thing I would do when I got home would be to collapse on the rug. I would be fast asleep for a period of time before getting up and starting to prepare tea. I had the two kids who I would bring home from nursery before Celia got home. This particular day had been a bad day at work. I got some bread, made some sandwiches and wrapped them up in a piece of greaseproof paper. I went and got three empty bean tins and filled them with water. I put all this under the table. There was one for my son Dean, one for my daughter Sharon and one for Celia. Celia came in and asked me if I had got tea ready. I told her that it was under the table because "that's how I had mine today and that's how you're having yours". Celia shouted the kids and told them, "Your Dad's going out of his mind". It had just got to me.

I went through these difficult periods at work where I would have bad heads, even ending up in hospital with it. It was all stress. I was also refereeing at this time and had a third job in a local pub doing three nights a week. I enjoyed working in the pub a bit and started to think whether it was an outlet to help me get out of the pit. Harry was the landlord of the pub which was called The George and Dragon and when he answered the phone he would say, "I'm George, the Dragon's upstairs in bed". Celia worked in the pub too. We actually looked at a couple of pubs to potentially run ourselves in Platt Bridge. In those days, the breweries would only offer you old, rundown pubs if you were new to it. We had our own house by then and there was no way Celia was leaving our house for a rundown pub.

My week was busy to say the least. There were times on a Tuesday night when the Floodlit Cup was on that I would also be travelling big distances to referee games at places like Whitehaven and Hull, getting home early hours of the morning and up at five o clock to go to work.

The stress of working in the pit, refereeing and working in the pub made me ill for five years, and I ended up with ulcers. I had terrible stomach problems.

Due to shift work, I couldn't get to some of the referee's meetings. I wanted to try and get a regular day turn at the pit. The management knew I was doing well as a referee due to reports in the newspapers and the colliery monthly paper *Miners News*. I went into see the manager and asked him if I could get a regular day turn so I could make referees meetings. He said, "I'll put it this way, you've got your mining which is full-time and you've got your refereeing which is part-time. Make your mind up, what do you want to be, a referee or a miner?"

I replied, "I'll tell you what, I've put a hell of a lot of time into mining and I've put a hell of a lot of time into rugby too from playing to refereeing. It's not happened overnight, I played rugby from 17 when I started at the pit and I've played rugby for the Coal Board in competitions. I don't have time off work, can you compromise and let me continue in both fields?"

"Nah, make your mind up whether you want to be a pitman or a rugby man."

I still had to do the two shifts until a job became available as a training instructor in mining. That was regular day work and was at Old Boston Colliery in Haydock. Old Boston had once had a fire and they'd had to flood it to put the fire out. They still had some pipes coming up the shaft. They used the gas that came off to heat the water for trainees.

It was a training centre for new lads coming into mining so they could be taught all the safety aspects of the job. I was on less money than what I had been getting but I didn't grind my teeth or jump in my sleep anymore.

7

Making the Grade

I remember very little about my debut first team game as a referee when I went to Leeds where they were to play Hull. I was very apprehensive. Headingley was a big place to go to with a vast stadium and a large, flat pitch. Many of the playing surfaces in Yorkshire weren't level, two of the worst were Dewsbury's old Crown Flatt and Batley's Mount Pleaseant – and that was a misnomer if ever there was one because pleasant it certainly wasn't!

So, going to Headingley for my first top level game was a big thing for me. Hull had a hooker called Flash Flanagan. In the tunnel as the teams were lined up to come out, I was walking through them I heard Flanagan say, "Hey, we've got a new ref tonight," as if I was there to be taken advantage of. First scrum, I blew up and gave Leeds a penalty. "What's that for?"

"New ref tonight pal, just letting you know, brand new".

"Alright, got the message".

That's what sticks in my memory about that night. I thought I came through it pretty well. The crowds were huge back then, I look back in amazement at crowds like 30,000 to see Leigh versus Wigan. Leigh are down to 1500 watching them now, it's sad.

Just as everybody had nicknames down the pit, I got the nickname "Max" when I was reffing from some spectators after the comedian Max Wall, or from the less friendly: "You little Lancashire bastard".

It was very hard getting up the ladder as a referee. You relied on the marks you got for your performance from the clubs you had refereed. The winning club would say you weren't so bad but the losing club would say that you were horrible. You were also marked on how smartly you were dressed. I see some of the officials today and am amazed at what they get away with. One of the touch judges recently came out with boots that were still dirty and I told him, "If I was your assessor, I would knock you 10 marks off for that before you got out onto the pitch". Our boots had to be black with white laces in. The first thing I would do after every match was to take the laces out and get them in water to get the muck out. It was a winter sport and you would get filthy. I would give my boots spit and polish; something we were taught by the top referees before us such as Eric Clay and Dennis Davies. They were the ones who set the standards for us. There would be a hanky in your top pocket also.

I did hit a problem when I grew a moustache as the powers that be didn't like it. I had grown it for a fancy dress party where I went as a Mexican so the moustache hung down a bit. The party was at Astley, about five miles from where we lived and I went wearing a sombrero and a sheepskin waistcoat with a pair of flip flops on. Celia was with me and we were quite young then. We had gone in a taxi. We didn't take cars as there was a drink on. I was really enjoying this party and making good use of some strong white wine frome Yates Wine Lodge. Somebody said, "The best way to drink that is in a glass with a bit of warm water and a spoonful of sugar". It was to my liking. But as the night progressed I had much too much to drink. In the early hours I was swaying around with a bottle of wine when Celia came up to me and asked, "What are you doing?"

"I'm having a drink," I replied.

"You don't have to drink out of the bottle, put that bottle

down."

"I'm enjoying myself, I'm sick of you."

I then decided that I was off. I looked at my watch to discover it was two o clock in the morning. I started walking it from Astley, nothing on my feet, wearing a sombrero and a Mexican outfit.

I had walked about two miles in my bare feet, got to the middle of Atherton where the streets were empty at that time of the morning when a police car came driving up, went past me then screeched on the brakes when I had obviously been spotted. They must have gone, "What the hell's that?" The policeman got out and said, "Pedro".

"Yes sir".

"Where are you going?"

"I'm going home."

"Where do you live?"

"Atherleigh."

Now in Atherleigh was a big old folks home. "Do you live in the home?" he asked.

"Clo ... Clovelly Avenue," I eventually slurred.

"Where've you been?"

"I've been to a party in Astley."

"I'll tell you what," he said. "It's been a bloody good 'un. What are you doing on your own?"

"Fell out with wife so I'm walking it home."

"Keep on walking and take things easy."

"You couldn't give me a lift could you? My feet are killing me."

"Sorry Pedro, I'm afraid we're not allowed."

I got another mile further on when second car pulled up, this time it was Celia, my mate and his wife. They asked me if I wanted a lift but I was still sulking so I said no. I had walked it this far and could quite easily manage the last couple of miles. I reflected for a second and then said, "But on the other hand yes".

The day after I found out I had broken my toe through

kicking a kerb. That was a good party. I liked the moustache so much I thought I would stick with it for a bit. I refereed a few matches like that. We had a director at Leigh called Bert Hulme who was also on the management panel at the Rugby Football League. He came to me one night after training at Leigh and said, "Stan, shave that tache off". I asked him what for and he told me that it didn't look right me refereeing with a tache like the one I had. He told me I was doing quite well but the tache would not help take me forward. I argued that it was nothing to do with the way I was refereeing the games. He insisted for my own sake that the tache should go. My marks came through and they weren't so clever. I had been marked down on my appearance. It came off and my marks went back up. I still pay attention to appearance these days and that's why I don't like some of the shirts modern officials wear.

There were a lot of things wrong with refereeing at the time, and we had to buy our own kit. So the selection of jerseys was whatever you picked. I ended up being the president of referees and for uniformity I decided to do something about it. I mean, once I actually went out in all white, everybody was gobsmacked. I used to play tennis a lot so it was all white gear. I thought it looked pretty smart and I knew it wouldn't clash. Someone said as I headed out, "He looks like he's stepped out of the washing machine".

Fellow referee Gerry Kershaw got involved with us trying to have set kit and I decided to try and get a sponsor. I eventually got in with Umbro who agreed to sponsor us, which was a big step forward. We then had uniform kits to choose from.

I remember years later when I joined the backroom staff at St Helens, club chairman Eric Ashton told me to go to the shop in town and get measured up for a club suit. I noticed that referees were turning up before games in whatever they wanted so I helped to introduce a dress code. This was a blazer with grey flannels. I even spent hours designing a referees badge to go on the blazer. We then had our own identity. It was another step forward. I always had pride in my appearance.

There were things passed down to us by older referees such as Eric Clay. He was a big lad and there was a confrontation with a player at Leigh once where he pulled the player to him, the player squared up to him and Eric just bumped him away with his chest.

I remember being a linesman once at a game at Knowsley Road. Clay was there and said to me, "Hey little lad, you can learn a lot off Eric Clay but be a little lad, Stan Wall, and make your own mark. I'm sure you can in your own way". It was his way of telling me to be myself.

8

Training with Leigh

When I started refereeing, I still went to Leigh every week to do my training. Celia would still be in the bar with her friends and it was a great club at that time. Great players like Geoff Fletcher, Frankie Barrow and Tony Barrow were tremendous characters. I trained with some great people there such as Don Gullick. The coaches I trained with at Leigh from my early 20s were incredible. I particularly remember Tommy Bishop who was very enthusiastic and bubbly. I also struck up a good relationship with Alex Murphy. Whenever a new coach came to the club I would always introduce myself to them and explain how I had trained with the club and ask if it would be ok to continue with that. I did all the running with the players and when they were running through moves I would be a body in the defensive line. At the end of each session I always joined in the tick and pass games which everyone enjoyed.

Training was nothing like it is now. There was no such thing as an all weather pitch. We had to go on the terracing under the stand to do steps. I'll never forget running up and down those steps. You then had to find somebody your own size, get on their back, then it would be up and down the steps like that. Then swap over and do it again. I'm sure we wore the concrete out of those steps at Leigh. Even when I was later involved in coaching at the club, we still did that. One of the steps was about four feet wide so that was used as a sprint lane. We would zigzag all around the Hilton Park ground going up and down the steps.

One part of training would involve kick offs from the centre spot for players to practice catching the ball. The ball was kicked towards me and not thinking, I jumped up enthusiastically for the ball. As I stretched my arms up for the ball, Tommy Graney came in and whacked into me. I finished up with a couple of cracked ribs.

Leigh had ex player Les Pearce as a coach for a spell, When we played tick and pass, Les would always put himself on one side in the game and was always determined to score. On one occasion the game had been going on for ages and Frankie Barrow bellowed, "For Christ sake, let Les score".

Les scored and yelled, "That's how you do it boys. Right, let's head in and get a shower".

On the subject of Frankie Barrow there was one match he was involved in where Billy Thompson was reffing. Billy always had a short, back and sides haircut. He'd penalised Frankie, Billy went back with the defensive line while the opposition was lining up their penalty kick at goal. Frankie looked at Billy and said, "Billy, who's cut your effing hair? I wouldn't let him cut our dog". In those days, refs weren't miked up so only they could hear it. Geoff Fletcher and Bob Burdell at Leigh wore wigs. The fun in those days was far different than what it is in the game today. Players really took the mickey out of one another. One night, the players came in and the two wigs were on the benches with four eggs in each.

As a coach, Alex Murphy was one of the best ever motivators. When Leigh won the cup final against Leeds in 1971 after being massive underdogs, it was Alex who made them play out of their skin that day. They were nearly hitting each other in the dressing room they were so fired up. It was all built up on emotion.

I went to Wembley to watch that game and that was an experience in itself. I managed to get four tickets as my kids, especially my daughter Sharon, were well into rugby by this point. Lo and behold, we were sat right in the middle of all the Leeds speccies. There was my kids dressed in the Leigh colours, but give credit to the people around us, they were having a joke with the kids saying they would probably be going home at half time. Leeds were red hot favourites for the game as they had a side of internationals. My lad Dean was insisting to them that we would win. They had superstars of the likes of Hynes, Atkinson and Holmes.

Alex could motivate people who weren't top players to go beyond the limits of their capabilities. That day, Leigh took the game by the scruff of the neck. I watched the game on DVD recently and it was like World War II. It was such a physical game, really dirty at times. Peter Smethurst got smashed time and time again in the final but always got up with a big grin on his face. He wasn't a dirty player, he was just hard. He had his nose broken umpteen times throughout his career; it was all over his face.

When Leigh got in front, Dean and Sharon started shouting their heads off. One of the Leeds fans had told them that if Leigh won he would give them half a crown each. He was as good as his word. It was a day of all days for us.

The players brought the cup back to the Town Hall on the Sunday. Celia and I were invited. Like all town halls, they had some lovely displays in there, palm trees and flowers. Guess what, when the players were going home, these displays ended up in the boots of their cars. The club received a letter from the council instructing the players that they had to return them all. There was some rum goings on that day.

After that the final the club decided to take the players to Lloret in Spain for a break. They played hard and drank hard. Now this was in the days of the Germans throwing their towels on the sun loungers. The lads had been out on the drink and came back to the hotel in the early hours.

They decided to strip off to their underpants, some dived in the pool. The others started passing them the tables, the chairs and the sunbeds. The players then set all these out on the bottom of the pool. They even put umbrellas up on the tables under the water at the deep end. It was hilarious.

Another night one of the players was seen swinging off a chandelier. The players ended up having to have a police escort back to the airport. The chairman, my friend Brian Bowman, said he would never, ever take a group of players abroad again.

Back then, referees weren't allowed to referee fixtures involving their home town club. I was glad about this as I would have ended up being biased against Leigh. The only time I was allowed to referee Leigh was the charity game they had before the start of the season. John Stringer would say, "You can referee us in this, we don't need to pay you then Stan," because money was so important to the clubs.

Whoever was refereeing locally at places like Swinton would come back to Leigh because after the game, we would be in the bar until 10 o clock at night. They just loved it.

All the players at Leigh then were ready for fun. We had two players: Peter Smethurst who was a butcher and Geoff Fletcher who was a pig farmer. Peter would come to training every Thursday night with sirloin steaks. Geoff would come and ask, "Who wants half a pig?" We didn't live cheaper but we ate more meat. I remember the first time I took one of Geoff's half pigs home; you got half the head with it too. My mum would make brawn out of the fat from the head. When mixed with water, it would solidify and it would be sliced up to be put on your sandwiches. It was horrendous. When I was helping with the coaching at Leigh, we once took our team to Dewsbury and after the game, they had dripping butties. "What the hell is this shit?" asked the lads. Dripping was just in the fat that came off when you roasted a joint of meat. As a kid, I once had condensed milk spread on my butties. Kids these days wouldn't be happy would they?

Leigh had some great players at the time. John Woods was a terrific player, very well balanced. His style of tackling was to employ the Cumberland throw and he had it off to a fine art. It might have been a Leigh thing as Tommy Martyn later adopted the technique. John was picked to play for England but was a really laidback lad. He really enjoyed going to the pub to play dominos with all the old fellas. John told Leigh that he didn't really want to be picked for the international game as it clashed with a dominos final. That incident would later come back into my mind when dealing with Paul Newlove at Saints. Paul was that kind of character too.

There was a guy in Bolton called Walsh who hand made rugby boots. Many of the players at Leigh and from other clubs would get these boots but John turned them down preferring a simple pair from Marks and Spencer's. For him, it really was a case of the boots not making the man but the man making the boots.

They wouldn't tolerate it today but all the players would dive into the bath after a match which would be full of blood and mud. The players loved that bath, and sometimes on a training night, they'd run that bath and put Radox in it.

All we had for recreation at the club was a table tennis table. When Alex came to Leigh, he loved his table tennis. I loved it too as I was a member of a table tennis team. I was born Church of England but changed churches because my local Methodist Church ran a table tennis league. I then changed to another Methodist church just like in the rugby, I was going for a better table tennis team. Before training at Leigh we would have a knockabout on this table tennis table but it got so serious with four or five of us that we would come to training an hour and a half before it started. I had a decent backhand; Alex was a pretty good all-rounder; Derek Higgs, the hooker, was good at chopping shots. We'd play these competitions then we'd go out to training. Some of the players would say, "He's bloody lost again at table tennis, has Alex". They could tell because training would be more intense if Alex had lost. "For God's sake, let him win" would come the cry.

We had been playing table tennis one day and Alex had a cyst right on the top of his head, it was as big as a pea. Physios back then weren't like they are now, they were more like first aid men. This guy we had, Hughie Bracken, told Alex he would take the cyst off. The physiotherapy room at Leigh was a shed, a little bit bigger than a garden shed. They had a couple of beds in it, an ultrasound machine and a heat lamp. Alex asked would it hurt and Hughie was assured him he would hardly feel a thing. Hughie said he would nick it then flick it out and stitch it up. We all piled into the shed to watch it. Hughie got his scalpel out and again Alex asked would it hurt. Hughie said it would be fine although he would feel a bit of something. Hughie didn't give Alex and anaesthetic, he just did it and Murphy squawked in pain. The cyst had come out though; Hughie stitched him up and then sent him straight out for training afterwards.

Some of the players who knew me from Leigh but went onto play for other clubs had the habit of calling me "Stan" during a game and I had to ask them not to. They could call me "ref" and you'd get "sir" a lot. Lads who knew you though would be shouting, "Come on Stan, give us a crack". Alex was like that when he moved to Warrington.

Every club had always brought in overseas imports but Hull KR started to bring over the better class of player from down under. Not only that, they started to bring in new innovations into the game. I refereed them one day and they got a tap penalty and some of the players would form a wall with their back to the opposition. The ball would go to the first man in the wall, then it would be passed between the men in the wall which would then open up and a player would run through.

I was training at Leigh at the time and having seen it, I thought I'd mention it to Alex. It was a good idea because the opposition didn't know which player had the ball. Alex came up with a few ideas and they worked on it in training. They decided they would use it in that Sunday's game. I had no match to referee so went to watch the game. They got a penalty and formed the wall, Billy Thompson was refereeing and he blew up saying, "I'm not having any of that, scrum down".

We went in the board room after the game and Billy simply said, "Oh, I can't be arsed with that". I always thought you shouldn't cut things like that out because it's good to see players and coaches thinking of something new. It's like years later at Saints when John Harrison headed the ball over the line, they stopped that soon after. To me, that is stopping people who are thinking.

Another thing Hull KR did was they had a penalty kick about ten metres in from the touchline and the kicker put the ball down ready to kick but all his forwards went over to the other side of the field. Instead of aiming at goal he cross kicked it, one of their taller forwards caught the ball and scored.

Another time I was refereeing Wakefield and Neil Fox was their goal kicker. I gave Wakefield a penalty about ten metres away from the opposition try-line. Neil came over to me and said, "I'm not kicking at goal" but pointed towards the sticks as if he was. He made the mark in the ground as if he was going to put the ball down to kick it. He tapped it, went over and scored. The opposition players went mad at me, "He said he was kicking at goal".

"Did you hear him say he was kicking at goal?" I asked.

"He pointed".

"He could have been picking his nose. I didn't put the touch judges behind the sticks, did I?"

It was good thinking by the player. He was a brilliant player.

9

Tales from the Disciplinary

I sent Jim Mills off in my first international game. It was England versus Wales at Salford in 1974. The captain of England was Roger Millward and the captain of Wales was Dave Watkins. Mike Coulman was propping for England up against Jim Mills. In those days, the first scrum was all about forwards trying to physically assert their authority on their opposite number. Everybody who knows the name Jim Mills knows the reputation he had. At the first scrum in this match, Mills and Coulman had a bit of a do. As the game went on, they didn't get near each other much. There was another scrum though and Jim whacked Coulman with his head as he packed down. There was a dust up, a bit of fighting. I pulled both players out with the captains and I said, "They've had a go early doors, they've just had another one and I'm not putting up with it. They either cut it out or I'll have to do something about it."

Jim said, "Yep, no problem Stan".

There was another scrum and Jim brought the nicest punch up from the floor you'll ever see and whacked Coulman. He flattened him. I had no hesitation and said, "Jim, you've been warned in front of the captains, on your bike". It was a tough game in those days.

The consequences of that was that he had to go and face the disciplinary panel. He appealed against the sending off simply because Widnes were going to Wembley. If he got three matches, he would miss the Challenge Cup Final. Jim appealed and I got a letter from the RFL asking if I could come to Leeds on the Tuesday night to attend the appeal. Now for me to attend I had to get permission off work. Jim didn't have to get permission from anybody. You had so many days you could have off work; they were called rest days. I had to take the appeal date as one of my rest days. I went to the Rugby Football League and it was the first time I had been. It was like a doctor's waiting room with me and Jim sat there. "Hi Stan, how are you going on?" he greeted me as I walked in. We had to wait our turn.

When I'd attended Referee's Society meetings I had been advised that if I had sent someone off, I should keep my report plain and simple. I shouldn't put too much in or the panel might be able to pick things out of it. I can still see my report now, it was about eight lines long. We went in the room. David Oxley was the secretary; the panel was filled with former players with cauliflower ears and various club directors. There was Jack Grindrod from Rochdale, hard as they come.

Me and Jim were sat in the middle of the room, side by side on two chairs with no table. It was like David and Goliath me being sat next to him. Jim was up to the ceiling and I was sat in his shadow. Jim was very jovial with the panel, "Hello David, alright Jack".

David Oxley offered to read my report to Jim. "No, you're alright Dave," said Jim. David Oxley went through it briefly anyway.

Jim responded, "Look, I'm telling you straight, I'm not calling Stan," and he put his arm round me. "I'm not calling him for sending me off, he was right. You know what it's like Jack, you have to sort one another out when you come in. Me and Coulman had had a bit of a dust up. We later had another do and Stan warned us. We came into the scrum and I did hit him. So I'm not blaming Stan for sending me off but I don't think Stan saw what happened first. As I went into the scrum, Coulman butted me and brought his fingers up and gouged me. Jack, what could I do? I hit him in self defence. I had to do something but I'm not blaming Stan. He was stood away from the scrum whilst the scrum half put the ball in. Gentleman, it was self defence."

The panel asked me if I had anything to add, I had always been told not to add anything so I said no. Anything I added verbally would be questioned as to why it wasn't in my original report.

The panel asked us to leave the room whilst they discussed it. We stood up and as Jim reached the door, he turned and said, "Jack, honest, self defence".

We sat down and I asked Jim, "Where did you get that from?"

"Stan, I had to tell them something didn't I?"

We waited for about five minutes when we were called back in. David Oxley said, "Jim, I'm sorry but you've got two matches".

"That'll do me David," replied a clearly delighted Jim shaking Oxley's hand and patting him on the back.

We walked back to the car park and Jim told me how happy he was to be available for Wembley. I asked Jim how much he had got for travelling to the disciplinary. He told me that the club had paid him. I told him all I was allowed to claim was second class rail fare. Chapeltown Road in Leeds wasn't near a railway station then so you had to go in your car. I had also lost a days work. I made my mind up there and then to never go to the disciplinary again. It was an experience going though.

Jim had been at Widnes, done his spell in Australia and he finished up playing for Workington. One particular day Ronnie Campbell was the referee. Ronnie lived at Widnes as did Jim. Ronnie had asked Jim if he minded giving him a lift to the game. Jim said that was fine. They went to Workington and the game kicked off. Pretty soon, Ronnie had to pull Jim out and tell him to keep his tackles low. There was then a scrum where fisticuffs broke out. Again, Ronnie had to speak to Jim and explain that he couldn't keep putting up with this. Jim did something again and so Ronnie told him that if anything else happened, he would have to send him off.

"Have you brought some money Ronnie?" asked Jim.

"What do you mean, have I brought some money?"

"Because if you send me off, you'll need some bus fare. You'll be bloody walking it back from Workington."

I later worked as assistant coach to Eric Hughes and he told me loads of stories about Jim Mills. There are stories of Jim hitting players in the tunnel before the match had even started followed by a remark of, "You'll get a bit more when you get out onto the field".

The great Vince Karalius went to coach at Widnes for a spell. Jim would listen to the coach but he was his own man. Jim was sent off once after about twenty five minutes into a game. Vince was furious, playing the rest of the game with not just a man short but a top international forward. At half time Vince went storming into the dressing room looking for Jim. He found him sat in the bath.

"Jim, have you got a bloody problem?"

"I'm glad you asked, this sodding water's freezing".

My mate Brian Bowman used to sit on the disciplinary panel and told me numerous comical stories including one about Mick Morgan from Castleford who was sent off for a stiff arm tackle. Mick told the panel, "Now you're not going to believe this gentleman but a mate of mine in the crowd shouted my name and I went to wave to him and my opponent ran into my arm".

Another was about Chris Caisley who was a solicitor as well as chairman of the Bradford Bulls. He came to the panel defending one of his players and introduced himself as, "Chris Caisley, chairman of the Bradford Bulls and solicitor". Jack Grindrod, chairman of the panel replied, "Jack Grindrod, chairman of the disciplinary committee and effing wagon driver," as Jack had a haulage firm.

Back then, the filming of non televised games was nowhere like how it is today. You'd just get someone at the club with a camera filming the game. These could be used to review incidents in the game. There was one involving Featherstone; their coach Paul Daley was a rum lad and a former scrum half. He went to the disciplinary to support his player. You had to go with your own video and have it ready at the point of the incident in question. They went through the report and then allowed Paul to put the video on. He put it into the machine and Omar Sharifcame on screen to the opening music of *Doctor Zhivago*.

"What's going on Paul?" asked the panel.

"I'll bloody strangle the wife," he replied.

She had taped over the game with the film. Paul was known as Omar Sharif from that point onwards.

10

Tales of a Referee

I was refereeing at Salford who were playing Saints. The Saints team arrived and about twenty minutes later Eric Leach, the Saints kitman came to me and said he had left the skip with the players boots in back at the club and he would have to go back to Saints to get them. As it would take him at least an hour to make the return trip I said I would postpone the kick off until he arrived back and the players were ready.

In the waiting period, the Saints players got dressed ready apart from their boots and I informed the Salford team and the press as to the situation.

The pressmen asked how long the match would be delayed, my reply was, "We'll start when they've got their boots," as we didn't know how long Eric would be with traffic. A very embarrassed Eric arrived somewhat later and we kicked off about twenty minutes late. I felt sorry for him as I knew him as he had been a former referee.

We had a meeting of referees once. We didn't have a code of conduct like today where they stipulate that you have to be at a ground so long before the kick off. In this meeting, they were telling us we should be there an hour and a half before kick off, and we were saying that you could go to places like Whitehaven and an hour before kick off the ground would be empty. They would all be in the pub. Then twenty minutes before kick off the place would be full. Billy

Thompson asked, "What about Huyton? It's like Fort Knox, it's all locked up. There's no glass in any windows, it's all boarded up. Last time I went there, they pinched one of the wheels off my car". Another referee had been banned from driving and had to cycle everywhere; he was on about locking his bike to a telegraph pole in Huyton. In the end they did implement a code of conduct that said the referee should be at the ground an hour and a quarter before kick off.

I was refereeing Huyton at home to Wigan as Wigan had gone in the second division. I got there and was first at the ground. I'd sooner be early; I am always on edge on a match day, even to this day. I don't go the toilet as often as I did then. If I do, it's because of my age. Geoff Fletcher who was a great character, was in charge of Huyton at the time. I was waiting and Geoff turned up with a big, "Alright Stan, I'll not be a minute, I'll unlock the gates". He let me in and showed me to the dressing rooms. He offered to bring me a cup of tea and I told him not to worry about it. He came back a bit later and told me we had a problem, he had just opened the gates to the pitch and some of the corrugated Asbestos roof had blown off the stand. He said, "Don't worry, we can overcome it. When Wigan come, we can get them to line up along the try-line with my team and walk across the pitch clearing the debris". He wanted me to ask Wigan when they arrived.

Geoff was flying around like a blue arse fly. He did everything at Huyton. He was player, manager, caretaker, the lot. You'd spot some crap in your dressing room and he'd be there with the brush.

Wigan came and I remember we'd had a lad come to Leigh called Dennis Boyd. He was a great player. He was hard as nails and a real tough nut. Dennis came and the first thing that players do after dropping their bags in the dressing room is have a walk in the pitch to have a look at the playing surface or to just stretch their legs if they had been on the coach for a while. Of course at Huyton, there would be no spectators there at this point. Dennis Boyd looked around and said to me, "What the bloody hell am I doing here today?" I replied, "There's another problem as well". I told him about the roof. All the players did in fact line up with myself and the touch judges and we were picking pieces of roof up. Geoff was made up as he really wanted to get the match on.

We hadn't been playing long when there was a knock-on and I blew for a scrum. Geoff was playing prop that day. I heard a frantic cry from him of, "Stan, Stan, come here quick". I rushed round to him and he said, "Put that in your pocket". He still had his wig on. In the heat of everything he had to do, he had forgotten to take it off.

That's not the funniest thing I put in my pocket. Whilst still an amateur referee at Marsh playing field in Leigh, a young lad came to me and asked me to put his glass eye in my pocket. I ended up telling him to give it to someone stood on the touchline for fear of it falling out of my pocket during the game.

Another incident involving Geoff was when Huyton came to Featherstone. The referee had to be given the team sheet before the game. Geoff came up to me and said, "Stan, we've only got twelve men, I'm putting A.N. Other on the wing". I asked him if the A.N. Other was bringing him up to twelve and he said it was twelve men plus A.N. Other. I asked him who the mystery player was as generally A.N.Others in those days were rugby union players who didn't want to get banned for playing rugby league.

"It's the bus driver," said Geoff.

I couldn't believe it especially when I saw the bus driver who was vastly overweight. They had put a forward's shirt on him and I think it was the first time he had had a pair of boots on him in his life. Geoff had somehow persuaded him to play on the wing at Featherstone.

When he took to the field, the Featherstone crowd who

were predominantly coal miners were delighted. They were all roaring with laughter at him. As the game went on they were demanding that the ball be given to the winger. He never got a pass for ages. Eventually, he did get a pass and they buried him. I bet he couldn't drive the team bus back.

Another time with Geoff was at York where it was wintry conditions. As I neared York I felt certain that the game would not be able to be played. Everywhere looked frozen. There were several unwritten laws amongst referees such as the ten metre rule for dissent (which was never in the actual rule book), that if both teams want to play a game, you should play it. It was ok for me as I would only be running on the frozen ground, not being tackled on it. If one team wanted to play but the other didn't then the referee would make the decision as to whether the game would go ahead.

Huyton got to York, on the verge of being late. I said, "It's not fit to play on this, Geoff".

"Stan, we are playing even if it's like bloody concrete. We can't afford to come back to York again. Our finances will not allow us to come back again."

We discussed it with the captains. I think Geoff had told York that if the match was off they wouldn't be able to come back again. The match went ahead and miraculously nobody got hurt. There was slipping and sliding and a few bruised and battered bodies but no serious injuries.

I also refereed the 1984 John Player Final in those kinds of conditions between Hull and Hull KR at Boothferry Park. The match was televised, all the cameras were there. It had been snowing and the pitch was virtually ice at one end.

David Oxley came over with his permanent smiling face, "Hello Stan, not the best of days for playing rugby but it's not too bad".

Hull KR captain Roger Millward came over and said that one end of the field was like concrete. He asked me if I had looked at it, I said that I had and that it did seem a bit dodgy but I knew the match would go ahead. He told me he hoped nobody would get hurt which I agreed with.

Due to television being there, that game was never going to be called off. With it being winter rugby, players had to put up with playing in ice and snow. It was a cracking game in the end. A big character from that era was Mick Morgan. Mick was a pitman like me so we had things in common. Mick had played for a number of clubs. There was one game Mick turned out and his legs were black, I asked him about this and he said he'd come straight from a shift down the pit. He'd washed his hands and face mind you. Mick moved to Oldham and there are two stories to tell about Mick when he was there.

The first story was when they were playing at Hull. At the time, Hull had one of the first Frenchmen to play rugby league in this country by the name of Patrick Solol, a winger. Dave Topliss was captain of Hull at the time. Mick could do a bit with the ball, and would sometimes run out wide. On this occasion Mick was running towards Solol when he turned his back and offloaded the ball. Solol came in and whacked Mick across the face. I blew up and pulled Solol out. I was talking to him when Dave Topliss came over and said, "Stan, he doesn't understand a word of English". By this time, Mick Morgan had come over to us and was wiping a trickle of blood from his nose. Mick interrupted, "I'll tell you what Toppo, if Stan doesn't make him understand, I'll make him understand whether he knows English or not".

The second story involves an Oldham player from Leigh called Terry Bilsbury. From training in Leigh, I knew Terry like I knew my brother. I gave a forward pass against Oldham and Terry said, "Stan, it wasn't a forward pass that". A little later I gave a knock-on and Terry again said, "Stan, not a knock-on that".

I said, "Terry, I don't care what you call me but leave the Stan out. Sounds too familiar".

Anyhow, Mick Morgan comes over and says, "He's not talking to you".

"What do you mean?"

"He's talking to me".

"Mick, how long has your name been Stan?"

"Michael Stanley Morgan."

"Piss off," I said.

In the bar after the game, Mick came over and said, "Let Michael Stanley buy you a pint". Mick was another who would always refer to me as 'Max' too.

Dave Chisnall was another big figure in the game. On one occasion I refereed Dave when he played for Saints at Hull KR. Dave could run; he was a fast player for a prop. Roger Millward had made a break, and Dave come across from nowhere and nailed him. It was a really good tackle. He got up and gave Roger a few verbals. Millward shoved him so Chissy butted him. "You little shit", bump and he was down. I had no option but to send him off. They are the decisions you don't mind as at least they are easy.

In 1980 I was reserve referee for the Challenge Cup Final between Hull and Hull KR which Gerry Kershaw was in charge of. The match fee for Wembley was £24 plus second class rail fare. We would get hotel accommodation but that was for a single room. We all took our wives so we had to pay for them. I ended up out of pocket. We never made any money through refereeing.

Gerry Kershaw was very nervous before Wembley and I tried my best to gee him up. We had one touch judge from Lancashire and one from Yorkshire. In the dressing room, if you wanted it, you could listen through a speaker to what was going on outside on the pitch. The music came flooding in from the pre match entertainment of on *Ilkla Moor Baht 'at* which the Yorkshire touch judge joined in with and then *She's a Lassie from Lancashire* that the Lancashire touch judge sang along to. I sang along too more to break the tension in the dressing room and help Gerry with his nerves.

At half time, it even got to the point that he didn't even know if he could go back on or not. I ended up rubbing him down.

The officials for the final all went out for a meal to a posh restaurant after the final. We are northern lads and the food they had in the menu had to be explained to us. Jackie Greenhalgh asked for a steak. They then brought out the raw meat they were going to cook to show him. "Hang on mate, I want it cooking," he said and he was serious too. I had to explain they were just showing him the cut of the meat. We had great fun that night.

I had trained with Alex Murphy during his three separate spells at Leigh. He left Leigh to become player-coach of Warrington, and this meant I could now referee him. I'd always had a good relationship with Alex. I got my list of fixtures I would be refereeing in the next month and I saw that I had Hull v Warrington at the Boulevard.

The week before Warrington were playing Whitehaven on a Sunday afternoon at Wilderspool. I was a rugby fanatic. I ate, slept and dreamt the game; I would often go watching Salford at The Willows on a Friday. Where there was a game, I would go so I went to watch Warrington this day. After the game in those days, you would go into the director's bar. Alex came in, spotted me, said hello and asked me if I was coming into the boardroom to have a drink with him. A bloke called Ernie was behind the bar and Alex asked me what I wanted. I said I'd have a gin and tonic so Alex said to Ernie, "A double gin and tonic for Stan".

"Just one's enough," I insisted.

Alex drifted off and I was chatting to some other people, when he came back he said, "Hey, you've got us next week at Hull haven't you?"

I said, "I thought you'd never bloody mention it".

He asked me if I was used to driving to Hull and I admitted that I wasn't. He said I could come up with them on the Warrington coach. It seemed a good idea to me at the time because back then I think the motorway only went as far as Huddersfield. I told him that it wasn't a bad idea but it wouldn't look very nice me arriving at The Boulevard in front of the Threepenny Stand spectators on the Warrington coach. "I can't do that Alex," I said. "I'd be fearing for my life."

"Don't be stupid, I always drop the players a mile from the ground. You can get off with them but don't walk in with them."

"Bloody hell. You think of everything you Alex. There's one other thing though. What happens if I send you off during the game?"

"I'll drop you off at the same place going back, a mile from The Boulevard and you can walk it back".

I ended up taking my own car and I'm glad I did. As soon as the game kicked off, anything that didn't go Alex's way and he was into me. If I penalised him for offside I'd get: "Come on Stan, give us a crack". A forward pass would be met with "Bloody hell Stan, never a forward pass". Eventually, Warrington did win.

The fog was setting in and I was worried about finding my way back. Alex said that I could follow the coach in my car. They were stopping off in a pub on the way back for a drink or two which was part and parcel of the game in those days. After leaving the pub after about an hour, the fog had really set in. I was following the coach bumper to bumper determined not to lose it until I got back on the motorway. We were coming through Pontefract and the coach went through a set of lights as they were changing. I followed and went through. There was police car on the other side who stopped me. He went through the rigmarole as I explained that I didn't know my way back to the motorway properly and had been following the coach. He said he had to do me. It's the only time in my life I've ever been done for a motoring offence. I think it was a ten quid fine. Worse than that, I had lost the coach. I ended up getting home in the early hours of the morning.

It could be hard work but there were some fun moments.

I remember Derek Higgs' testimonial at Leigh and near to the ground was a British Legion club. After the match, Derek was having a do there. Referee Ronnie Jackson went to it and it was one o clock in the morning before it all ended. Ronnie lived in Halifax and when you go over to Yorkshire, there is a road with a reservoir on the right hand side that descends into Rippendon. I was worried about him getting home at that time.

The next morning I decided to give him a ring to make sure he was ok. His wife answered the phone and I asked, "Is Ronnie in?"

"Yes, he's in, he's in a right bloody mess, he's covered in blood."

"Was he in an accident?" I asked.

"I'll put him on".

"Hiya Stan, I was coming down Rippendon Road when I hit a sheep so I put it in the boot. We've lamb chops now for the next six months".

11

Escaping Odsal

One of the biggest incidents of my refereeing career took place at Odsal. It was a 1981 Challenge Cup tie between Bradford Northern and Widnes. It was a very hard game in muddy conditions. Odsal hasn't changed much over the years, the main difference today being that the dressing rooms are now level with the ground. Back then, the dressing rooms were at the top of the ground. That meant climbing 97 railway sleepers to get up there. You'd walk down around 30-odd steps, across a macadam bit then go down the rest of the sleepers to get to the pitch. You had that walk through all the spectators. It wasn't too bad coming down because the game hadn't started. There'd be a few little jeers such as, "Come on you little Lancashire bastard, are you going to give us a crack today?"

Jeff Grayson was playing for Bradford at the time. He had never been to Wembley. There were some great players who never made it to the Challenge Cup Final such as John Woods. This day, the two packs of forwards tore into each other. Widnes had some star players such as Eric Hughes and the Mylers so were the favourites. Bradford though were winning 8-6 right on the death. Myler broke through for Widnes with only the full back Keith Mumby to beat. Myler chipped the ball over Mumby's head, Mumby stuck a leg out and tripped Myler. The decision had to be a penalty where the ball bounced. This meant a kick for Widnes to level the scores under the posts. They kicked the goal and it was 8-8. In those days, they went with the referee's watch to decide the end of the game. I blew the whistle for time, the Bradford players were around me upset at the penalty but it really had been a clear cut decision. The Widnes players were as 'chuffed as a butty' at escaping with a draw. They knew it would be a replay at Widnes on Wednesday night.

Five policemen came onto the field to me, all Bradford police and Bradford supporters. The chief inspector said to me, "Tell you what mate, you've made it bloody hard for me to get you off this pitch up them steps".

So I said to him, "I'll tell you what mate, I've done my job here. I had to give what I saw. Now your job is to get me from here up them 97 steps and in that dressing room".

They didn't even bother about the touch judges. They got left to their own devices. I got to the bottom step and the crowd were mental. I had the chief inspector up front and four coppers around me. I was making my way up the steps in this little cage of police whilst the spectators were baying and spitting at me. I got to the little macadam junction and when I got there, there was a police horse. The horse was in front of me and had to walk across the path to the next lot of sleepers. It was on a bit of a slope so the horse was taking its time to make its way across. It suddenly stopped dead and had a crap at the same time as the police were trying to push me forwards. The crowd was delighted at this with cries of "Yeah, you always were a little shithouse Wall".

The horse eventually veered off and the policeman got me going up the next lot of steps. When I got close to the top, the little cage of policemen around me broke up a little bit. A girl took a swing at me. Her punch caught me a glancing blow on my shoulder. I got into the dressing room and let out an almighty sigh of relief. I was drained and not just from the running about on the muddy pitch for eighty minutes. There was the mental drain from all the hard decisions made during the game not to mention the walk up through the crowd.

The chief inspector came in and told me he had the girl who had hit me and did I want an apology? I told him no, it was ok, it had only been a glancing blow. He asked me again if I wanted an apology and again I said no.

"Yeah, you do," he insisted. "I'm telling you that you do". He wanted to bring her in. The young girl came in. She was only around 17 or 18 and she was close to tears. She was clearly worried sick. "I'm sorry, I'm sorry for what I did." I just told her the main thing was for her not to do it again.

If you were a referee at Odsal and Bradford had lost, you had to endure that every time. The referees asked the RFL to do something about it but they said all they could do was get the policing right. The referees said that that wasn't good enough and that we shouldn't have to go through that. It got to the point that when you saw Odsal on your list, you'd start to dread it. What they decided to do was to take the referee down in a car. Back then, you could go from the dressing room down to the pitch by car. It went right out of the gates then back in via the speedway track. The first time they did this, it was an Oldham referee called Terry Keane. He was only a similar size to me. Bradford lost and the crowd turned the car over!

At half time at Bradford, you would either stand in the middle of the pitch or just walk to the side. There was nowhere else to go as an official.

There were problems in the game back then. I did once see at Leigh when a referee got kicked between the legs by a spectator after a game.

At The Willows, Salford, you only had to walk up a few steps to get to the dressing rooms but the crowd were getting onto the officials so badly that they had to put a bit of a fence up.

Naughton Park was another place behind the posts where there was a little cage thing you ran out of to get onto the pitch, you would always be covered in spit at Widnes.

At Huddersfield at half time, the teams wouldn't go back to the dressing rooms. They'd walk off the pitch to a little place under the stand where they could get into a huddle. Watersheddings was the same in Oldham. The referee would just stand in the middle of the pitch with his touch judges.

It was always nice to go to Halifax as they were nice people and always friendly. I had refereed at Leeds the week before in front of a capacity crowd. Now at Halifax, there was five hundred and a dog.

It wasn't a clever game this day and half time came along. I was stood in the middle of the pitch having a chat with the touch judges.

"Crap game this isn't it," I said. All of a sudden, I saw this little boy of about 10 years old come walking across the pitch to me.

"Mister," he said, "my Dad says will you put these on at half time?" whilst handing me a pair of glasses. I laughed at this and the lad walked off. I pretended to put them on and looked up at the crowd who enjoyed this. I shoved them in my pocket and we got on with the second half. The game finished and we trudged off the field back to the dressing room. I'd been sat down for about ten minutes when there was a knock on the door. The same little boy was there, "Mister, can me dad have his glasses back, he couldn't see the second half properly".

There was a write up in the paper over this little incident saying: "Referee sees the funny side". That's what is lost in the game today. I look at what I did and what I was involved with in those days and it was great. After a game, you could go in a bar with the players, even those who you had sent off, have a bit of a crack with the spectators. It was fantastic. It never happens today; players can't talk to referees.

I remember one incident with a touch judge. The dressing room for the officials at Hull KR was up a flight of steps. They gave you a key so you could lock it then one of the touch judges put the key in his pocket during the match. It got to half time and we couldn't find the key. We couldn't get into the dressing room so I told my touch judges that something would probably be sorted for us for full time. During the second half one of my touch judges came sprinting on waving his flag.

"Right, who was it?" I asked getting ready to speak to the culprit of whatever had gone on in the tackle.

"I've found the key," came the unexpected reply.

I was dumbfounded but had to improvise and call over the hooker and tell him to "cut it out".

When Saints went to Castleford during the 2013 season, a bloke spoke to me in the tea room asking me to tell his friend about the time I refereed Castleford v Widnes during the miners strike. The strike went on for so long that it split whole families up, brothers against brothers, fathers against sons. They had been getting food parcels to survive from places like Russia but it wasn't enough. Some started drifting back to work. A lot of pickets came from Yorkshire in coaches. They would picket Lancashire collieries. Late in the strike, people started to drift back to work in Lancashire before they did in Yorkshire. I remember refereeing that game and they gave me holy hell. They nearly tipped my car over by rocking it. They knew I was a Lancashire miner.

I had a fair few things to put up with as a referee but I still look back and think that they were great days. I suppose it did take a special kind of person to be a referee.

12

Travelling as a Ref

The warm up back in my refereeing days before a game for players was a glass of sherry. There would always be a bottle of Harveys Bristol Cream in the corner of the dressing room. Everybody drank out of the neck of the bottle, not like today when players insist on their own separate plastic cups – not that there's any sherry in the dressing room today. All teams used to have a bottle of sherry before a game, and there'd be two raw eggs in a glass. That bottle of sherry would go round the dressing room hand to hand, mouth to mouth. The players would also have hot baths back then and as soon as the first player got in that water would turn absolutely filthy. There'd be players with cuts so there'd be blood in the water. Once the players got out, you'd be washing half the pitch out of the bath with a hosepipe.

We used to have a referee and two touch judges in our room, but today there's also in goal touch judges plus a masseur. I never had a massage in my life. I was never injured whilst refereeing although often tired. I was working a treble life with the pit, the pub and the refereeing. I only ever missed one game as a referee at Wakefield due to fog on top of the Pennines which stopped me getting to Belle Vue in time.

Brunton Park in Carlisle was the biggest pitch you'd ever referee on, it was as big as Wembley. I did one Cumbria v Australia match there. They would always put a stuffed fox in the middle of the pitch which was the Cumbrian emblem. The Australian touring side were amazed at the size of the pitch. Of course, they ran the Cumbrians ragged. They threw the ball about as the big pitch suited them down to the ground.

Maurice Bamford was a very good motivator in the game at this time. When he was born, they must have c christened him with water out of the rugby league players bath. His heart and soul was rugby league. Now there were certain times a referee would go to a dressing room before a game to explain something to both teams. It might be that the referee would be cracking down on lying on that day. I was approaching the Huddersfield dressing room and I could hear Maurice – who was the then coach at the Fartown ground – on top note to his players. I thought I'd better not knock just yet and had a listen in instead.

"Right, we've been rubbish the last three weeks. I know it's effing lent and everybody gives something up for lent. Yours has been effing tackling. It's effing over now (he was banging on the table by this point). You get out there and you knock some effing heads off."

I refereed at Craven Cottage, Fulham. It was a good experience. Initially, they were getting gates of around 11,000. I went down there once for a game between Fulham and Leeds. I was down to referee on a Sunday but the weather had been very cold with a severe frost for several days so there was concern about the playing surface.

The RFL rang me and said they wanted me to go down on the Saturday and inspect the pitch. I drove down and before I went to the hotel, I went straight to the ground. The groundsman let me in and I put my boots on. Craven Cottage, much like Knowsley Road, had one part of the ground that never got any sun at all. Unlike Knowsley Road, the ground backed onto the Thames rather than the Crispy Cod. That side of the ground was like concrete, and to be fair it wasn't much softer anywhere else. I used to use my car key as a prodder to test the pitch and it wouldn't go in. The groundsman came over and I asked him what the weather forecast was. He told me they weren't allowed to speak to referees. He said this was down to soccer where they weren't allowed to influence referees in any way. I told him that we weren't talking soccer, we were talking rugby. I asked him what the ground would be like at 3pm the following day and he told me it would be the same as it is now. I told him the game was off but just as I was saying that, a young bloke walked on the pitch carrying a plastic shopping bag under his arm. He said, "Mr Wall, my uncle has sent me down".

"Who's your uncle?"

It turned out his uncle was one of the directors at Leeds and he had wanted his nephew to go on the pitch to test it out and see if the game was playable. He asked if I minded if he put his boots and I told him he could please himself. He ran up and down, didn't slip and said, "It's not too bad is it".

I said, "Ok, what we'll do is you can run at me a few times and I'll smash you on the floor then we can see if the pitch is too hard."

"No," came the reply. "He just asked me to have a run on it."

"Well go back, ring your uncle and tell him Stan Wall said the match is off".

They had obviously wanted to play the game. I had driven all the way to London for a half hour pitch inspection then had to drive all the way home.

When the Southend side came into the game, I had to go and referee them. Whilst I was down there, they gave me another match to do on the same weekend at Fulham.

By this time, Fulham played at the White City Stadium, a venue with an athletics track around the pitch. I did the Southend game, had a night in a hotel then had to referee a night game at White City. It was Fulham versus Cardiff Red

Dragons. The weather was bad and we waited and waited for Cardiff to arrive. We eventually got a phone call to say that they were on their way. It was one of those games that had to be played due to the distance between the two clubs. Cardiff arrived and I asked them for their team sheet, it had 8 A.N. Other's on it. I told them that I couldn't send that to the Rugby Football League and that they would have to put names to those players. They were reluctant to do this as many were rugby union lads who would have got banned for playing league. Eventually 'names' were put to players and we kicked off around quarter to nine at night. There was a sparse crowd in the huge stadium. I said to myself, "What am I doing here?"

At half time, somebody brought the officials a big chocolate cake in. That was a bit out of the ordinary.

During the second half, a bit of a brawl erupted. I had to go in and sort it out. I looked up at the clock and it was nearly quarter to eleven by this point. I just said to the players, "Look at the clock, let's just get this game over with and get out of here, nobody's watching and you're wanting to fight".

We had to travel home after the game so I only got in during the early hours of the next morning. There were flowers everywhere in the house. I said to Celia, "Oh, I didn't realise it was mothers day".

She went berserk, "Mothers Day! Do you not realise it's our anniversary?"

I had forgotten completely. Rugby again, it was always in my head. Rugby always came first with me.

At one time I went down to referee a game in Cardiff and me and my touch judges on the Sunday morning decided to have a look at the Millennium Stadium as we were particularly interested in the trophy room we had heard about. We went down in our blazers and ties, looking very smart. We asked the guy on the door if he minded us having a look at the trophy room. He started to say that was ok but then twigged the emblems on our blazers and said, "Oh, you're rugby league boys aren't you?"

I told him we were and that we were up for the game later that afternoon. He said, "I am very sorry, you can't come in".

I asked him what the reasoning behind that was and he told me that they just didn't associate with rugby league. I said that was terrible and asked him for his name as I was going to write to my MP about it. He told me it wasn't his doing and that he was only carrying out orders from the Rugby Football Union. He then said he would sneak us in for a quick look. I told him to sod off.

It was sporting apartheid, discriminating against us just because of our sport.

It had happened over the years, I know Kel Coslett had been back to Wales trying to get lads to sign for Saints, and they wouldn't dare say in pubs why they were there. It was big deal between rugby union and rugby league.

I refereed two internationals in France, one in Villeneuve which is a lovely place. They left me to my own devices as a referee when I went over. I wandered around having a look at the beautiful town. I wandered into a big hall one day which was like an indoor market. Everything in this market was alive, all the chickens that you could buy, they all had their legs tied together so they wouldn't fly off. I'm not sure how popular fridges and freezers were in France at the time so what you could do was take a couple of hens home and leave them in the back garden until you were ready to eat them.

There was one thing that sticks in my mind about the game itself which is something of a staple of French rugby. There was a brass band in the crowd which played during the game. When the side they were supporting had the ball, they would play a fast tempo but when the opposition had the ball it would slow to a waltz. It was an experience.

They were never easy matches to referee; the game in England was ruthless at the time, dirty up to a point. I'd always ask my touch judges to watch for anything off the ball as we didn't have the advantage of television replays. In France, the players seemed to take a step further and would kick or even bite on occasion. One fellow referee advised me before my trip, "First thing to do when you get there is start digging yourself a tunnel out of the dressing room as the crowds could get very angry towards officials".

On the whole though, I found that it wasn't too bad. My other international over there was in Perpignan. That went so well that they asked me back to do their cup final. I stayed with a guy called Julien Rascagneres, who was their best referee at the time and came over to England to referee some international games. I flew to Paris, where he picked me up and he drove me to Perpignan. He lived with his wife and two children. Julien didn't speak much English but his children were learning English in school. He worked as a postman. I asked if I could come with him on his round one day. It was an interesting experience. We got up early, a lot of buildings in the town centre were five storeys high. We'd go through the front door and there'd be five boxes. Julien not only took the post out but he also paid pensions to some of the people as well. He'd ring the bell and the occupier would let us up.

Halfway round, we called in a barbers shop. Julien knew the barber so we stopped and had a cup of coffee. When we finished with the post, he took me to the market where he bought food for the evening meal. He told me we would have escargot (snails). He bought a huge bag of about 100 live snails. Julien's wife cooked the snails in garlic butter

They eat barbecue style a lot in southern France. His wife worked but would come home in her lunch time which was a siesta break of a couple of hours. She would use that time to prepare everything for the evening meal. She would be marinating pork chops and so on. I really enjoyed the lifestyle over there. I found that they were very sociable people. Wherever I went, I would be offered food and hospitality. I went back to Perpignan a few times.

Once, myself, Ronnie Campbell, Gerry Kershaw, Sam Shepherd and Joe Manley went over to Perpignan for a meeting with the French senior referees for a week long conference. We stayed in a beautiful area near the beach. One day, we had a free afternoon after lunch. Gerry Kershaw got stuck into a bottle of wine over lunch and decided to head for a sunbed. I did have concerns about Gerry in the sun considering his skin was akin to that of a ghost. He fell asleep in the sun and I told Ronnie we should put him in the shade.

"Sod him," came the less than concerned reply.

Ronnie Campbell and myself had a walk down to the beach. We returned after about an hour and Gerry was pretty much cooked by this point. We woke the bright pink Kershaw up. He couldn't move properly. We had to put him in a cold bath of water. He spent the rest of our time there smothered in calamine lotion.

Perpignan is all about the vineyards and is on the edge of the Pyrenees. There is no heavy industry there. When Rascagneres came over to England and because he had been so nice to me, I was wondering where I could take him in the area. I was working as a trainer at Parsonage Colliery at the time so I decided I would take him down the mine. He was absolutely terrified. He'd come from such a lovely part of the world to an area of heavy industry. He then had to get changed into safety boots and a safety helmet. We then went seven hundred yards deep into the bowels of the earth. He did enjoy the experience though at the end of it all. It was probably one of the biggest things he ever did in his life.

There was another group of people I once took down the pit. In the era when Nat Lofthouse was involved at Bolton Wanderers as manager of the club, the team were losing matches and Lofthouse was none too pleased with the players. He arranged for his team to go down the pit. The team came to the colliery and I gave them a briefing before we went down. I explained about the dangers of the pit. We kitted them all out with the necessary safety gear. I asked what was behind Nat's thinking of bringing them to the mine. He said, "Well, they're not playing well,the spectators are on their back, and I've told them that the spectators who watch them work very, very hard. The people on the terraces are working their hearts out every day. They come to the club to spend their hard earned money to watch the team. I told them that I wanted them to go and see what the spectators had to do to go and earn their money to see if they appreciate it."

I thought that it was a great idea. For anybody who has never been down a mine, it is one hell of an experience. Some were terrified, especially when they were at the metre high coalface. They were crawling on their hands and knees through the dust and heat.

At the end of it all, Nat thanked us for what we had done and told the players, "That's the kind of thing the spectators have to do. Now if you don't work hard at football and make a success of it, it will be this type of job that you will have to go for".

The downside of it was he then invited me, my mate and our wives to watch a match at Bolton. To this day, it remains the only professional football match I have ever attended. They wined and dined us, we had a lovely pre match meal but it was a terrible game that ended 0-0. Nat came to us after the game and asked if we had enjoyed ourselves, I told him the meal was superb.

"Sorry, I couldn't do anything about the match," he replied.

13

Dealing with the Troublemakers

I would get a month's worth of my rugby fixtures in advance and would eagerly read it to see which nightmare players I would have to contend with in the coming weeks. The strategy back then for sides was to take the opposition's best man out, by any means necessary.

Paul Woods from Cardiff was always one to watch out for. Len Casey at Hull KR was another. Eddie Szymala at Barrow, covered in tattoos, was one more. Every team had players like these. You recognised them by their mashed noses and cauliflower ears. You knew a game with Jim Mills in it was always going to be hard work.

As a referee, I would go into the dressing rooms and check the players, they'd hold their hands out and you'd make sure they had no rings on. If they had long nails, they had to have them cut. You'd examine their boots too. If they had any strapping on, that too would be checked. The ones that really needed to be looked at were the players who had strapping on their forearms. Some of the players were crafty though and after being checked would re-strap sometimes 'loaded' forearms.

It's easy to send a player off; you blow your whistle, show them the card and that's that. It's far more difficult to keep them on. We were always told by the older referees to work hard to keep players on the field. We would be told if there was a certain player to watch out for, to stand at the side of him in the defensive line. You could then keep in his ear about keeping his tackles low.

Some you couldn't help though; players who would gladly belt someone off the ball. I would always tell my touch judges to be my eyes off the ball. That was difficult for them at times as it's human nature to follow the ball. There was only five yards back for the defensive line from the play the ball in those days.

Barrow had a scrum half called Arnie Walker, who was one of the hardest lads you'll ever see yet was only ten stone something wet through. He was picked to play for Cumbria against Australia at Derwent Park. Ray Price was playing for Australia that day, another really hard case. Arnie caught Ray with a jumping high tackle and wrestled him to the ground. Ray got up, played the ball and spat on Arnie Walker's face. I had never, ever seen that happen before and blew the whistle straightaway. I brought Price over and told him, "I've been refereeing a long time and I've never seen such a disgusting act. That was diabolical".

He said, "The little pommy bastard nearly bit my effing finger off". He had deep teeth marks all around his finger. Obviously you couldn't see someone biting in a tackle on the floor.

Alan Hodgkinson was a Leigh lad who played for Rochdale. I knew him personally from living in the town. Wigan had brought in a very raw winger by the name of Green Vigo. In this incident, Vigo was scooting down the wing whilst Alan was coming in on the angle towards him. As Alan got close to him, Vigo turned inside him. Alan caught him flush with the elbow as he did so. Alan just said to me, "You don't need to tell me, I'm going". Vigo's teeth had come through his lips, I don't think they were wearing gumshields at the time.

One of the hardest things I had to do as a referee was to

send the great Neil Fox off. He had never been sent off in his career. He was playing at York at the end of his career. This particular day, they were playing Rochdale. The Hornets had a hooker called Peter Clarke who would always put himself about. It was towards the end of the season and if York won, Hull would go up. As Hull weren't playing that day a lot of their spectators had come to the game to watch it. Neil Fox was playing stand off and was doing a good job. He wasn't just a big lad, he was a good ball player as well.

When the second half started, I could see from the Rochdale players that something had been said to them in the dressing room at half time. They were all trying to nail Neil Fox.

Fox turned his back to let the ball go and Peter Clarke caught him with one hell of a whack across the jaw. He dropped Fox to the ground. He then jumped up and chased after Clarke. Unfortunately Clarke fell and Neil just put the boot into him. All the other players fired into it and there was a scuffle. After I had separated the two sides and restored order, Clarke was still on the floor, putting in an Oscar winning performance with his cries of, "Where am I? What day is it?"

"I'll tell you where you are, you're off," I told him.

"Who's head and ball is it?" he asked.

"Peter, you're off, get off".

"Alright Stan," he said getting up and walking off.

I then had no option but to go to Foxy who had never been sent off in his long and illustrious career because he was a gentleman player. I had to send him off. I know he later said it was a blight on a spotless career. The consequence of all this was that Rochdale went onto win the match once Foxy had gone off.

In the bar afterwards, Clarke admitted to me that they had been told in the dressing room they had to sort Fox out.

One of the biggest incidents in my refereeing career was a Lancashire Cup 2nd round match at Knowsley Road between St Helens and Warrington on the 14th of September 1983. It was a night match and the atmosphere was electric. The problems started when Warrington winger Phil Ford deliberately stamped on a Saints player. It set World War III off. It was right in the corner of the ground. Everybody ran in. Players were flying in from the other side of the field like missiles. The brawl involved all of them and it moved right up the perimeter wall where I'm sure a few of the spectators tried joining in. The police had to get involved to calm things down. It took an age to sort out. I took a deep breath and tried to assess the situation. The touch judge nearest to the incident was able to give me some help but the one on the far side had just stood there really enjoying it. I pulled Fordy out and sent him, Mark Forster, Roy Haggerty and Steve Peters off. Both sides were down to eleven men as a result.

Straightaway, Warrington forward Mal Yates was laughing and gobbing off at a Saints player when he punched him. "Not again" I thought. I launched in as quick as I could and sent him off too so Warrington were now down to ten men. Both sides started playing rugby a bit then because there was so much space on the field.

In the bar after the game, Warrington coach Kevin Ashcroft, who was someone who always had a lot to say for himself said, "Bloody hell that was some fight. How did you manage to send five off?"

"That was the easy part," I replied. "I didn't know which ones to leave on".

Derby days on Boxing Day would always be tough whether it was Warrington v Widnes or St Helens v Wigan. I remember a Wakefield v Featherstone match I refereed and it was a battle royal. There was Jimmy Thompson, Keith Bridges and old Harold Box, who could clean players out. Both teams were at one another from the word go. That was another coalmining area so a lot of the players would work together. There was blood everywhere. After the match, as my heart rate finally calmed down and I went into the bar, I saw Mick Morgan with blood trickling down his face yet holding Jimmy Thompson's baby on his knee. They were all the best of friends once the game had finished.

I remember one game where Hull travelled to Headingley to play Leeds. Two players had had squared up a number of times during the game so I eventually had to send them both off. The Hull coach Arthur Bunting wasn't happy about this. After the game, he came and knocked on the dressing room door. He came in and started effing and blinding at me. I told him that I worked in an industry where such language was second nature but when I came home to my wife and kids I never used it. I told him I was happy to discuss anything with him but let's discuss it on a proper level. He wouldn't shut up. I told him I had offered to answer any of his questions but if he wasn't happy with the way I had refereed the game, the proper way of addressing it would be to get a pen and paper and write a letter to the RFL. I said that all the names under the sun that he had called me would be going into a report about him. I then had my shower and went into the bar. Bunting came across to me and apologised for having a go at me and that it was in the heat of the moment. I told him I accepted his apology and left it like that. Neither of us reported the other one. We got on really well after that incident. I have even seen him socially in recent years and was invited with Celia to a function at his house. Things like that show how special the game is and why those who love it will always do so. Out of it all comes friendship.

I refereed Wally Lewis' first game for Wakefield. He got £1,000 a game and played ten games. Whilst over here he scored six tries including a hat trick against St Helens. Wakefield did well whilst he was over here but when he went home, their form dipped and they ended up getting relegated. His debut at Wakefield was a complete sell out, it was against Hull. Even I was excited about going. We've had some good stand offs in our game such as John Holmes at Leeds who was a terrific ball player. Wally Lewis had incredible hands though. I felt good after refereeing in that game. Apparently, he had doubts over whether they would pay him the money as he was coming to the end of his career but they did so he came and honoured his contract. I was fortunate to referee some real legends of the game. Refereeing those types of players were nice moments in my own career.

When I was refereeing, I was invited down to London to speak to the Rugby Union Referees Association. Joe Manley also came with me. They had sent me a letter saying they felt that they could learn a lot because they were having trouble at the time. Whilst we were down there, we also went to a meeting of officials from a variety of different sports. Everybody looked up to us. We couldn't believe some of the stories we heard from other sports. At Wimbledon, the tennis officials couldn't get in a lift at the same time as a player. They were having issues at the time with John McEnroe smashing rackets and shouting at umpires. Soccer was going through hell at the time with players following referees across the pitch when they had made a decision.

We then went to the rugby union meeting and we came out of it really well. They wanted to know how someone like me at five foot nothing could go up to a giant like Jim Mills and give him a telling off yet still be respected by the player. They loved our rule of moving players ten metres back for answering back. The soccer referees were saying they wished that they could do that. They said they got terrible bad language from the players.

I once refereed a game at Oldham, they had a young kid playing for them who was at me verbally all first half. On the way in at half time, he came up to me and started having a right go coming out with the f word. I told him to stop it. He carried on so I told him he was off, he had been sent off at half time and wasn't to come back out. I asked him his name and he said, "Effing Donald Duck".

I included that in my report along with his real name that I got from the club secretary. Donald Duck ended up getting about four matches.

As for facilities then, I was amazed the first time I refereed at Elland Road. I went into the referee's room and it was a lounge. It had a three piece suite in it and a drinks cabinet. It had a little changing room part too. I asked why it was so plush and the officials explained that the soccer referees couldn't go into the bar afterwards with the players; they had to stay in this area. I think that's how rugby league is going today; it's becoming an us and them situation which is no good for anybody.

Elland Road was the exception as we had some horrendous referee's rooms. I think when most grounds were built, they forgot the referee needed a room. Then before the first match, they'd realise their mistake, take a toilet out and convert it into an officials room. The St Helens one was like that. At Leigh, the room was under where the stand sloped down so you couldn't actually stand up in the bath.

At Doncaster, it was a little room adjacent to the pitch. Inside was a coal fired stove, you'd light it to heat the room. A little old man came in to light it for me. I had to leave the room, the smoke nearly killed me. The fumes came out everywhere as the chimney wasn't jointed properly. The people were so hospitable at Doncaster though. The people who ran that club had massive hearts. I was refereeing there one match and my mate Brian Bowman said he would come there with me as he knew the two directors there. Their directors' room was amazing. It was a tiny caravan behind the stand. Despite yet another Doncaster loss – they were going through a horrendous run at the time – I was invited into the caravan after the game. They had a bottle of whiskey fixed onto the table with an optic on it, same thing with a bottle of gin.

It was fashionable in board rooms at the time to drink whiskey and milk. It ended up with about twenty people in this tiny caravan enjoying the whiskey and milk in the middle of winter.

It was always nice to go to Headingley, but they had their problems though as the officials room had a door that opened into the home dressing room. Very often, I'd be getting changed only for a Leeds player to come in, "Alright Stan, can I go on the shithouse?" He'd sort himself out and leave me with the smell. Good old days!I always called players by their first names yet some other referees felt that was too familiar and we should call them by the number on their jersey. My argument was that in winter rugby, you often couldn't see the number. I remember refereeing once at Oldham and being flattened by a tackler who thought I was one of the opposition. He apologised and I didn't do anything about it.

Referees used to decide when to end a game originally, then the RFL brought in their own timekeepers to do it. Each club would have their own person with a stop watch. The issue with that is if you both go to stop a watch at the same time, it will inevitably be fractions out. There were debates on when to stop the game and what to stop it for. Also, there was no set hooter system across the grounds. Some places would have a bell. Billy Thompson at one referee's meeting said he had gone to Whitehaven and, "They had two bloody dustbin lids banging together to end the game".

I was at Leigh once when the hooter failed. The Leigh secretary John Stringer came sprinting down from the stands to tell the touch judge to stop the match whilst the game was still going on.

Wakefield came up with a system which I thought was good, a green and red light system. When the referee put his hand up to stop the clock, the red light would come on. Everybody then knew the game was stopped. The referee waved his hand again and the green light would come back on.

The system wasn't working well everywhere though and

it became a major problem. At referee's meetings there was concern that it just wasn't working. The best solution would have been for every ground to have had an electronic system but not all of them could have afforded it. It's so much better today for the speckies when they can look at the electronic scoreboard at a ground and see exactly how long is left.

The RFL now send ex referees and touch judges to time each match. I should be doing it because they get £100 a game. Not bad considering I used to get £12.50 for actually refereeing a game.

As for other referees of the era, I always admired Fred Lindop, who was one of the top referees. He reminded me of Alex Murphy in that he was always immaculate. He was a perfect build and his signals were done with precision. He was a good disciplinarian.

John Holdsworth was a bit younger than me, coming up through the ranks. He went on to do very well in the game even though he sometimes struggled with his weight. He was another good referee.

14

Compulsory Retirement

Tragedy struck the refereeing world when two referees died. We were left to our own devices to train. I was fortunate in that I was able to train with Leigh. I never carried any weight on me. I prided myself on being quick. Some referees would just go out and do street running. I would do terrace runs and sprint at Leigh against Kenny Green, I would always want to beat him as I still had that competitive edge to me.

Joey Jackson, a Yorkshire referee had a job that took him overseas. He had been abroad for quite a few weeks in the close season. He then refereed a pre-season friendly at St Helens, got changed, went up into the tea room and dropped dead.

The RFL then introduced measures to check the referees out. This led onto referees having to go to Salford University under a guy called Gerry Quinn and do a medical. They wired us up and put us on a treadmill and ran us until exhaustion. They monitored us whilst doing this but pushed us to our limits. When you got off the treadmill, they would have a graph of that run which showed your heart rate.

They would also wire us up and monitor our heart rates during an actual game. They would then compare the treadmill graph to the game graph. Now, on the treadmill, the only stress you had was exhaustion. On the game graph, there would be physical stress but also the stress of making decisions or splitting a fight up. During my game graph, my heart rate had peaked around three times, on each occasion it was over the maximum. The way they explained it to me was by imagining a car. You can drive comfortably in that car at seventy miles per hour. If you push that up to a hundred miles per hour every so often, it could blow a gasket.

Another referee on the treadmill at this particular time was Mick Naughton from Widnes. Whilst Mick was running, they stopped the treadmill. They had noticed that his heart rate had been going up and down during the run. They told him that he had an irregularity with his heart. Now Mick was another top referee. He had taken charge of some top games including internationals and had never had any trouble. They told him for the time being they didn't want him to referee. He went back for another test four or five weeks after and the same thing happened again. They told him he would have to stop refereeing. He stopped for about a year then asked could he go to another independent person to redo the test. The doctor reconfirmed the same problem. It was suggested that he might be able to continue refereeing at a lower level but they wouldn't even really advise that. He started up refereeing at a lower level and he dropped dead.

It's led onto the situation today where the tests for referees are far more strict. We went from running on the treadmill to doing sprints to doing jumps. They now test for body fat. There are people who more easily put weight on than others. I was lucky; I had to get a bruise to put weight on. Now referees have gone full-time, there shouldn't be any unfit referees.

If I had gone full-time when I had the opportunity, I'd have thrived as I was always a glutton for training although I'm sure a lot of that was down to the fun element of training at Leigh. They brought in that you had to run so many laps in so many minutes so I found myself training down the East Lancs Road which I found very boring. If you've got someone to compete against in training, it spurs you on. I loved that side of it. Alex Murphy used that a bit in training; he would have me sprinting against the scrum half Kenny Green. You would have to lie on your stomach, jump up and sprint. I would always have one knee under myself ready to run. Alex would yell at Kenny, "Greeny a bloody referee like him can beat you". It was all in good humour.

There was a mandatory retirement age of 50 for referees. I dreaded 50 coming round as I wanted to go on, I didn't want to finish. I'm still active today and I've always looked after myself. I always thought there was a place for us. Now they're doing it, they're involving past referees as assessors, match commissioners or video referees.

I always said that you were better when you finished than you were when you started. You'd be at the stage where you were getting respect off the players and your man management skills were finely honed. Some referees were former schoolteachers and took that approach into their refereeing. They couldn't man manage as well as the rest of us. They were talking to players like they were school kids. I'd be mixing with Leigh players after training who would be boasting about giving someone a crack in their last game. I'd see someone give a smack in a game and quietly say, "He's due one back," and once that happened that was usually the end of it.

Before Ronnie Campbell was given the 1985 Challenge Cup Final, I was told by a leading RFL official I had Wembley. I really built my hopes up as you can imagine. I'd already been reserve referee for the 1980 final between Hull and Hull KR with Gerry Kershaw being the match official that day.

Ronnie was a good referee, don't get me wrong but I was so disappointed when I didn't get the final. I ended up getting the Premiership Final the week after Wembley. Ronnie's final between Wigan and Hull was in my opinion the best ever. There was Ferguson and Kenny on one side with Sterling and Leulai on the other. He refereed it well.

Hull were the better team second half but just ran out of time.

One thing I did fight for was for referees to go up the steps at finals and receive medals. That hadn't happened previously with the officials only getting a tankard. I've got a loft full of bloody tankards. I argued that we were part and parcel of the game and that we should be presented to whoever was handing out the trophy that day. Eventually, the RFL listened to us.

I also helped to introduce referees assessors after games. It was previously done by the home team and away team giving you separate reports. You got a half decent report off the winners and a rubbish report off the losers. We eventually got ex referees to be assessors.

I'd been disappointed with missing out the week before at Wembley so the Mal Meninga Final as it is known was my last chance. As a result, I was really looking forward to it. St Helens and Hull KR were two good teams. Meninga was such a star and it was his last game for Saints. He's still a legend of the game. There were other great players in that game too such as Mark Broadhurst for Hull KR. It was held at Elland Road. I just hoped it went well for me, being my last game. It was a good game. There was some excellent tries scored. The standout thing, and I can still see it now, was Mal coming through hitting Gary Prohm with his shoulder, it was a real solid cruncher. He had such a huge frame. He also went nearly the full length of the field for a cracking try. I thought "I'm going to keep up with this guy'" and he could shift. If you look at pictures, I was always on the spot pointing for tries. I didn't need a video ref as I was always Johnny on the spot.

On occasions I would wait for the player to get to the line and say "'Where've you been?" as they scored. I didn't say that to Mal.

The Premiership Final in 1985 between St Helens and Hull KR was a great final. There was one aspect of my own performance I wasn't happy with. There was a kick through and somebody took Barrie Ledger out but I wasn't sure who. The touch judge didn't give me anything but it appeared there had been a raised foot. That's just my own critical self.

Saints had borrowed a hooker from Leigh called Gary Ainsworth, who scored from a pass the Hull KR players felt was forward. I saw Gary after the game and joked, "Bloody mile forward that, whilst you're a Leyther I gave it". You couldn't do that now but it was all part and parcel of the humour of the game. It helped you develop relationships with players. There was Harry Pinner playing with no teeth in and someone complained he had bit them, I said, "How can he bite you with no teeth?"

It was ironic that I later finished up at Saints as kitman. A lot of Saints speckies over the years have come up to me saying, "Great final that Stan". "Aye, great because you won," I reply. But it was a great game to finish on although the downside was me thinking "Have I finished in this game?" I hadn't though and the next chapter of my life in rugby league was about to begin.

That's the 19 year old me on the left hand side of the bottom row. I was playing for Wigan Road Working Mans Club Open Age Rugby League side and we had just won the Leigh and District's 7 a side competition. Yes our prize was genuinely a reading lamp

Mining was a big part of my life

At the back as part of the Mines Rescue team

Laying the law down to
Fulham's Ian Van Bellen

A proud day as I was
reserve referee for the
1980 Challenge Cup Final

The 1984 John Player Trophy Final
between Hull and Hull KR, not
the best of conditions!

On the spot to
award a try despite
the icy conditions

Dave Watkinson of
Hull KR getting a
talking to

At Salford Variety club after being named one of the top three referees of the year

My final game as a referee, the 1985 Premiership Final between St Helens and Hull KR, known as the Meninga Final

As a born and bred Leyther, it was an honour to be on the coaching staff at Leigh

Alex is someone I have always had a great deal of time for

My old boot room at Knowsley Road which was signed by many of the players

Celebrating Saints' 2000 Grand Final win with star centre and gentleman Kevin Iro

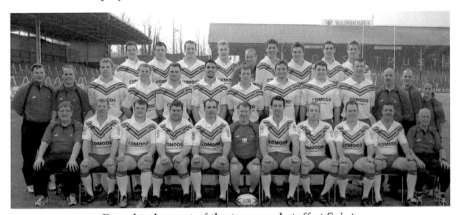

Proud to be part of the team and staff at Saints

2000 and another trophy, this time a Challenge Cup Final win over Bradford at a rain soaked Twickenham

Sean Hoppe, a true gent who would always lend a hand at training

The fans at Saints have always been great, they even made t-shirts about me!

2006 and before the side went on to win the treble, they travelled to Marbella for a pre season training camp. This was our Spanish themed night. Some talent in this shot!

I never dreamed I would end up on a GB photo, a very proud moment for me

Working alongside Andrew Farrell with Great Britain, I always got on well with him

On top of the world with two great Saints captains, Chris Joynt and Paul Sculthorpe

2004 GB training camp. I had been dressed in drag to the amusement of Brian Carney and my old mate Longy

November 2007 and another proud moment as I was inducted onto the RFL's Roll of Honour for lifelong service to the game

Me with Oliver, one of my great grandchildren

With my wife, Celia, who has had to live with my life long passion for rugby league

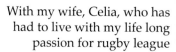

A great family event as Celia turned 80. Here she is with three of our great grandchildren Aaron, Oliver and Coby

My great grandchildren keep me on my toes, I'm playing here with Aaron and Coby

I've enjoyed writing this book, here I am with Oliver, the son of my co-author, Andrew Quirke

15

Moving to Saints

Prior to finishing my refereeing career, I had started sowing some seeds by going on coaching courses. I got my coaching qualifications as a result, I got my level two down at Crystal Palace. Later I went to Wigan under Graeme West and Phil Larder and did a weeks course and I got my level one under them. They brought into the game that everybody had to have a coaching certificate. You had long standing coaches such as Alex Murphy who had no written qualifications. The RFL insisted that everybody would have to go in for these qualifications. Alex was never going to go on a course. It has led to today where everybody has to go through the system which is only right.

I went straight to Leigh where we started building a different kind of relationship up. I had previously coached with the Colts there whilst refereeing; now I was assisting Alex with the first team. It was the club to go to for me.

Alex was in and out of the club as he coached a lot of different sides over the years including Warrington and Wigan. I was actually head coach for six weeks at Leigh. I was assistant to Alex and he had some sort of dispute with the club so I was put in temporary charge of the first team.

When weights started coming into the game, I set about to build a gym at Leigh. I wasn't into conditioning as such, not like now where it is such a specialised subject. We just didn't have that level of knowledge then. The first rugby league player to really get into weights was Vince Karalius. He was years ahead of his time. He had the biggest hands I have ever seen, like shovels. The weights he used were weights from the coal wagon. They certainly weren't barbells.

Tommy Dickens ended up coaching the side and we did quite well in the old second division. Tommy was the manager and I became the coach. I was coach for two years under Tommy Dickens and we got the side promoted. Coaching is just man management really. I never fancied being a head coach, I think it was too late in life. They asked me to be a referee's assessor but I always had this feeling in my mind that if they didn't referee like Stan Wall then I would possibly mark them down. I didn't want to be an assessor. I did feel like I could pass on good points to players though.

Whilst at Leigh, we had a player called Steve Halliwell who was an Australian centre. In one season, there was money to be given to the top try scorer. There was an understanding at Leigh that any man-of-the-match monies would be pooled into a kitty at the end of the season. Halliwell won the top try scorer cash but refused to pool the money and then signed for St Helens. Unfortunately for Halliwell we had some tough players at Leigh at the time and when the team played away at Knowsley Road the next season, the players made it right. From the kick off he was levelled. Everybody from Leigh was delighted at this. He could keep his money.

Eric Hughes later came to the club and he was there for a while. Eric had also been a good player but I always said to him that it would have been easier for me to send him off in the first five minutes of a game than leave him on for 80. He could be a bad lad hitting players just off the ball. He was a hard man and that was part of the culture of the game at the time.

Eric was then asked to go to St Helens whilst Mike McClennan was their coach. Hughes was put in charge of the youth side there. McClennan left Saints after an altercation with a supporter and Eric Hughes became the coach. He asked me to go and join him there as he would be getting rid of all the existing backroom staff. I became his assistant coach but it was a hard decision as I had been at Leigh all my life. I chatted to my son Dean about it and he was adamant that I go to St Helens as I wasn't as likely to win anything with Leigh. It was Dean who I took advice off more than anybody when it came to going to Saints.

So in January 1994 I started my time at Saints. They had players like Tea Ropati, Phil Veivers, Shane Cooper, Jonathan Griffiths, Sonny Nickle, Adam Fogerty, Jon Neill, Bernard Dwyer, Paul Loughlin, Alan Hunte, Anthony Sullivan and Vila Matautia. We brought Scott Gibbs and Bobbie Goulding in. It was a good era and despite it being a big change for me, I enjoyed it. Eric Hughes was a fantastic person. You couldn't meet a more enthusiastic coach. Today we have trained masseurs to give players a rub down. Back then Eric Hughes would massage every players legs before a game, all whilst motivating them. That was his way of doing things.

The main people in charge when I first started at Saints were Mally Kay, Eric Ashton and Tom Ellard. It was a very friendly club where everybody was treated in a friendly manner. Everybody was part and parcel of the club from the two old ladies washing the kit to the chairman. As for the players of that time, Paul Loughlin was a funny lad with a very dry sense of humour. He seemed to have a love for streaking. We once had a bowling competition at the Carr Mill pub on the East Lancs. The bowling was well under way when Paul streaked across the green.

Eric Hughes once arranged an Outward Bound course, which was just over Parbold hill. You had to climb trees and do archery. There was also a lake there with rafts on it. When it came time to diving into the water, Lockers decided it was time for him to do some skinny dipping.

Bernard Dwyer was another dry one; him and Lockers

were a double act. Gilmour, Pryce and Fozzard were the same sort of thing a lot later on. Bernard was a quiet kind of lad, a very hard player. When he got with Lockers, they became a couple of comedians.

Sonny Nickle was a fabulous person. He started off in the part-time era and was a fabulous trainer. He was a big lad and always pleasant off the pitch. We once had a young lad from Wales, a prop, come to us for pre-season training. Sonny was then getting on in years but left this lad for dead. We pointed out at the time, "If you want an example, Sonny is your man, that's the kind of fitness levels you've got to achieve".

We also brought in Apollo Perelini. I remember his debut against Oldham at the Watersheddings – an apt name for the place as it always seemed to be wet there. He came on as a substitute, eager to make his mark. He had a point to prove in a new game in a new country. He didn't last ten minutes before he was sent off. At the Watersheddings, the dressing rooms were in a big house from where you would then walk down to the pitch. I say dressing rooms, when they were more like pig sty's. When Apollo was sent off, I had to walk him back to the dressing rooms. He was upset so I was just telling him not to worry about it. He went for a shower so I told him I was going back to the pitch. Just as I got there, Sonny Nickle was sent off so I had to walk back with him.

Off the pitch, when I first started at Saints, we sorted out a new group of backroom people. We brought Brian Case in, the former Wigan prop, to work with the A team.

A gentleman called Jack Coatsworth worked at the club and as nice a guy you could ever wish to meet. He called everyone "Cockle". He always got dressed up as if he had come to work in an office. He was incredibly smart and came to the club every day. He was very polite and would ask if he could do anything to help me. He would offer to mop the dressing room but I couldn't see Jack mopping in a collar and tie, it wouldn't have been right. He was so helpful though.

We had another lovely man from St Helens called Ronnie Wright. He was a physio who had his own practice. He used to strap the players up. Then there was Brian Collins, the statistician.

We also had Billy Bates there who helped out with the A team and started doing stats for them. He moved onto being the kitman for the Academy. I'd get all the kit ready and he'd come and collect it. He also took one particular job over from Jack Coatsworth. Jack used to spend ten quid a week on toffee that he shared with everyone on coach journeys to games, earning him the nickname "Toffee Jack". Billy took this over when Jack left – not because it was a job that had to be done but because Billy Bates likes toffee. Unfortunately he'd spend ten quid on toffee and not give any away. If we were ever at an away game and didn't know where Billy was, we knew the first place to look would be the burger van. I'm joking about him here as I know he'll get a kick out of being mentioned in the book. In all seriousness, he has worked very hard for the club over the years. He did a lot of programme notes too. He has been a club stalwart. We had a good group there including Derek Jones, the masseur.

Eric was there two years but we didn't win anything. We came very close in the Regal Trophy Final against Wigan at Huddersfield but we were narrowly defeated. It was an excellent tackle by ex Saint Gary Connolly on Vila Matautia that perhaps turned the game. That was pretty much the end for Eric though.

Shaun McRae was Eric's replacement, coming in from Australia. To be honest, with Eric going, I felt they would get rid of me too as usually a new coach brings in their own people.

16

Equipment Manager

When Shaun McRae came in at St Helens at the start of Super League in 1996 he told me he would like me to stay. He explained that he was bringing in former Great Britain international Mike Gregory as his assistant but there was definitely a job for me. I think it ended up being called equipment manager and my job was to sort out all the training and playing gear requirements for the players. This also meant I had to deal with the sponsors. We brought Mizuno in which was a big deal at the time. They had never sponsored team sports before. Shaun MacRae also said that as an ex-referee there would be things I could see and explain to him that would assist him as a coach.

Soon after I started in the equipment manager role I realised I needed more help, so Alan Clarke came in to assist me. He had been working in the club shop on a voluntary basis. I asked him if he'd like to help me and he jumped at the chance because it meant being involved with the team. He's been a great help ever since. I was full-time at that point and was responsible for ordering kit, washing it, getting tackle bags ready for training and all the gear ready for match day.

I enjoyed the new role as I was still involved with the team every day. Again, Shaun was a great fella to work with. I still recall the first day he came to the club and it was snowing. He looked out of the office window onto the pitch to see a blanket of snow. "Stan, how do we train today?"

He had never encountered such conditions before so I explained to him, "It's dead easy. You pick two teams and we have a snowball fight".

David Howes was chief executive of the club at the time, the lads decided to bury his car in the snow. It looked like an igloo. He had to dig himself in to get home that day. Him being at the club led to really good things for me internationally later on.

We had great success under Shaun winning the Challenge Cup and the first ever Super League in 1996. Wembley 96 had been the first major trophy the club had won in 20 years. You couldn't have written the ending as a seemingly dead and buried Saints came back from 26-12 down with three Bobbie Goulding bombs being the catalyst for a 32-40 victory. A great way to win a game but it must have been difficult for our opponents, Bradford. Great memories, and we went back to Wembley the year after to win it again against Bradford.

It's always a terrific atmosphere going to Wembley. You go to the stadium the day before for a walk round to get the feel of the place. They won't let you train on the pitch but they do allow the goalkickers to have a couple of practice shots. Walking out into that silent stadium is quite an experience. I have stood in the royal box looking down onto the famous turf. On the day of the match itself, it's best bib and tucker with ties on. The big difference on match day is that all the crowd are in then. Going up to the stadium on the coach surrounded by your spectators is an amazing experience. The coach goes very slowly to work its way through the mass of people. You get off and everybody is wishing you luck and patting you on the back. I can't tell you how good the feelings are in those situations.

I'd then set the dressing room up but still have time to walk round the pitch in my suit.

Everybody mentions walking out of that old tunnel but it's a fact of life. The tunnel is in semi darkness and you can just see the opening. You come out and the bright sunshine and roar of the crowd take your breath away. Superb memories.

After that tremendous win in 1996, doing the lap of honour was sensational. Having my photo taken with so many different spectators. Then celebrating in the dressing room with the players.

They had the old fashioned plunge bath at Wembley back then, there was a five foot high wall surrounding the bath. The players urged me to get on the wall and jump in the bath which I did, I still remember Keiron Cunningham urging me on. You don't get that as a referee! The first time is probably always the best time. Having said that, I still think the cup final against Wigan that we won in Cardiff in 2004 was the best.

A part of the reason for the success was the world record signing of Paul Newlove from Bradford. To get Newy we had let three good players go: Lockers, Bernard Dwyer and Sonny Nickle. Newy arrived in a Securicor van at Knowsley Road, chained to a security guard in a PR move designed by David Howes. It was good publicity for the club. David had also introduced the popular club mascot, St Bernard, a role initially filled by his son James.

We also had Scott Gibbs who, when he came to the club, was overweight and out of condition. What a nice lad he was, very easy to get on with. He always had a smile on his face.

Club captain Bobbie Goulding had been outstanding in the 1996 final but there was an unpleasant incident back at the hotel after the game when he had had a few drinks. That was the other side of him. There were other incidents when we were away for the World Club Challenge and in Wales for an on the road game.

He was such a terrific player and yet had the other side of him where he could be quite a dirty player at times. I knew Bobbie long before he ever came to Saints. I had been on my coaching course and one of the junior teams in Leigh came to me. They had had players from being eight years old and were finding once the players reached 15 they were getting a little bit out of hand. They had become too familiar with the coaches they had known for seven years and needed something extra. So I went to Leigh Rangers and coached the under 15s. We did well, I think I put a bit of discipline into them and a bit more professionalism. At the end of the season, I organised a function at the Greyhound pub in Leigh for the mums and dads who had brought them every week and stood in the pouring rain. Through coaching that side, I came across Bobbie when he was playing for his junior side. His dad was with him and I had refereed his dad at Huyton.

After the Wembley success, we then won the first ever Super League title at Knowsley Road. It was a terrific period for Shaun MacRae, and of course, the spectators after two decades of waiting.

The following season, we got to Wembley again but not without a scare on the way. Bobbie got sent off when we played Wigan in the fourth round of the 1997 Challenge Cup. It was for a high tackle on Neil Cowie just before half time. We still beat them with only twelve men. Lee Briers deputised for the remaining rounds but Bobbie was back in the side for Wembley. You had to feel for Lee, I was really glad when he went to Wembley years later and won the cup with Warrington.

For the '97 final, the day before the game, club physio Janette Smith had turned her ankle. She was really upset about it because she wouldn't be able to run on the pitch. Give her credit, she somehow got herself right to do it and I'd never seen an ankle like it. No matter what capacity you were in, you wanted to be part of that special day.

The team at this time was a good one and included Alan Hunte who was a Wakefield lad. He was a pacy winger who scored some good tries for us. He always had a lot to say for himself. You do need those talkers in your team. Then you'd have your quiet ones like Sonny who would listen to everything.

On the other wing we had Sully who also scored some great tries. He was a very quiet man. He just went about his business. We would do bike rides to Southport, once we got there the lads would have a swim in the swimming pool, get something to eat, then load the bikes and themselves in one of Janette Smith's big horse boxes for the journey back to St Helens. Sully could never get in the back though, he was very claustrophobic. I don't think he was a fan of the smell of horse shit either. He sat in the front with me and Janette with the window down and his head stuck out of it like a dog. Sully also didn't like you squeezing a teabag in his cup either; he said it made all the tannin come out.

One day after training, Shaun McRae grabbed me and conditioner Nigel Ashley Jones and said he would take us to the KFC on the East Lancs. We got in his car. He switched on and I noticed on the electronic display that it said he had only five miles of petrol left. We got to Windle Island and it was down to three miles. I told him he had better get some petrol but he assured me that there was always some left in the tank. He carried on down the road and as soon as it hit one mile, the engine began to splutter and then died.

I berated him, "Well Shaun, I can't bloody believe that. You're an intelligent person".

"I thought there would be more in than that," he protested.

"How can there be more petrol? It was telling you. It's like a voice saying that you need petrol."

We were stuck on the East Lancs road with cars whizzing past us. He asked what we should do next, and I told him that the three of us needed to get out and push it to the nearest layby which is what we did. We then got on the phone to groundsman Neil Holding asking him to bring some petrol that he used in the lawnmower at Saints. It took him some time to fill the jerry can and then get to us so while we were in the layby, I kept shaking my head at Shaun telling him, "I wouldn't like to be in an aeroplane with you". There wasn't much petrol in the can but enough to get us to the KFC and adjacent petrol station. After we had something to eat, I pointed out the petrol station and Shaun replied, "We're alright, we've got enough petrol to get us back to the club". I made him get the petrol.

The English clubs had to take part in an expanded World Club Challenge involving some fixtures played down under. The Saints players all dyed their hair blonde on that 1997 trip. When I got to the airport, I didn't recognise half the lads. We went over there and first game was against Auckland. We got destroyed by them. The overseas commentators were loving it saying, "The guy with the blonde hair has dropped the ball."

I did have some good times with Shaun McRae during the 1997 World Club Challenge down under leg. Shaun had picked the place we stayed in at Coogee Bay. It was a fabulous hotel where he introduced me to oysters. One time, I saw a woman eat thirty of them. What I did learn about Shaun on that trip was that he is a big Elvis fan. One night we went into an Elvis bar and he knew every word to every song. That was a good night.

On that trip, we had the young prop Andy Leatham. One training session took place on a school playing field. He got bit by a spider and finished up in hospital with a very badly swollen leg. And to compound matters, Janette Smith had some prawns and I couldn't recognise her the day after because she had lumps everywhere due to an allergic reaction.

During the World Club Challenge in 1997, a gentleman who would play a huge role in St Helens' future by the name of Eamonn McManus looked after us. We stopped off in Hong Kong where he was a banker. He took us to the bank; we went up in a skyscraper. He wined and dined us all. He said he had two options for the rest of the day for us; one was for us to be taken on a short sightseeing tour and the other was for us to go and get a massage after being on a plane for so many hours. Nearly all the lads opted for the massage. It was only daft people such as me, Eric Ashton and Janette Smith who went on the sightseeing tour. We all met up later and swapped stories which was when I found out I had made the wrong choice as the masseurs had been attractive, young women.

Ellery Hanley followed Shaun McRae into the top job at Saints and spent a little over a season at the club. I was very apprehensive about what Ellery would be like. I had refereed him quite a lot as a player. He had been such a good player. He was totally different to Hughes and McRae. He was very motivational in his ways. He didn't mix with the players. He was the coach. The first training session with him was at Edge Hill College, Ormskirk. Training was to start at 10am. The club had a brilliant Aussie conditioner at the time called Nigel Ashley Jones. Nigel's mind was an open book so he and Ellery really hit it off tremendously well because of the professional attitude of both of them. You'd get to the training pitch and you'd think it was Manchester Airport as there were cones everywhere. I'd gone to Knowsley Road first as I had jobs to do there before training, and Ellery gave me a lift to Ormskirk in his 4x4. I said I would take him to the dressing room but he said no, he told me he was going up to the training pitch. About 9.55 the players started drifting up to the training pitch but a couple of them got there one or two minutes late. Ellery said, "I said training was at 10.00am. I'm only telling you this once. You all need to be on this pitch for ten o clock or you will have me to answer to". I agreed with him.

He would be very aggressive in training; the players would be split into teams to do competitive sprints against each other. If he saw a player encroaching over the starting line, he would make that team do another three or four sprints. Again, I had nothing against that.

We had sessions at Ainsdale on the sand dunes. If Nigel

set you a course out on there, you'd come off really tired. We had an Australian player come over to us at this time called Phil Adamson, brother of the more famous Matt who ended up coming over to play for Leeds. Funnily enough, even though he never played for Saints, I always had a really good relationship with Matt. It might have something to do with the fact that he wanted to swap a shirt once and I sorted it out for him. You have to remember that St Helens is a fashionable club and many opposition players are keen to get hold of a Saints jersey. The rumour was that Saints had got the brothers mixed up when signing Phil. He never hit it off with Ellery and he wasn't the world's best trainer.

After training, Ellery would always open two tins of rice pudding and put them in the microwave for himself then go and eat in his office rather than in the restaurant with the players.

In the dressing room every day, he'd have a big notice pinned up, which would very often be a motivational notice.

We played Gateshead away that season and went up the day before. We always took a doctor with us to games. We had a training session the day before the game and when the doctor wasn't there, Ellery hit the roof. It wouldn't have improved his mood to have discovered that the doctor was flying a kite on the beach. Ellery would never swear though, he had controlled aggression.

Eric Hughes came back to the club during the 1999 season in a football manager type position whilst Ellery was coach; there was public tension between the two. Ellery ended up being suspended from the club. The next home match was against Hull and the supporters were protesting about the suspension. There was some anger directed towards Eric. Some supporters had stayed behind after the game to make their feelings known. I was walking towards the clubhouse end of the field with a wheelie bin when one of the supporters asked was Eric in the bin and I had a laugh and a joke with them. I think it broke some of the tension.

The way kit used to be transported was in a huge whicker basket which was readily available due to the abundance of mills in the area in years gone by. They had four wheels on. They were low on the floor and were hard work.

When wheelie bins came in I had the idea of filling them with kit and transporting it across the pitch after a match. Other clubs took up the idea.

After games, you get supporters waiting for autographs, they often ask me where such a player is and I'll joke that he's already gone because I snuck him out in a wheelie bin. That's a key difference between rugby and soccer because many soccer players won't sign autographs.

We've sometimes stayed in the same hotels as Manchester United and apparently before their stay, the hotel staff are informed that they cannot ask for any autographs. They're not even meant to speak to them.

The worst ground to get away from is Castleford as the supporters there all want photographs with players and they stand in the actual doorway we need to get through to leave. I wouldn't change that for the world though. That's how it should be. One Cas lady asked if she could have her photograph taken with me and I said, "Yes love, I can still pull the birds then".

We got to the 1999 Grand Final, playing Bradford yet again. One of the things that sticks in my mind about that game was where Sonny Nickle tried to chase down Henry Paul and nearly stopped him scoring. It was a tremendous chase back. We later would see James Graham do the same thing in games, a never say die chase from a forward on a back. That was Sonny all over, a big heart and aggressive. He would never be put on. We always held him in high regard.

In the match, Kevin Iro scored out wide and Sean Long had a conversion out wide to put us in front. I always had a habit with Longy because of our relationship of telling him to take his time. Often he had scored the try himself and he was pumped with adrenaline. It was late in the game, he was out of breath, I took him his drink and cooled him down a bit. He said, "This is a hard one". I said, "Take your time, don't rush. If the referee wants to stop the clock, he will. You've got all the time in the world. You kick it when you are ready to kick it. Get your breath back". It sailed over and we won the game, we were champions again. After the match in 1999, Samoan Freddie Tuilagi literally danced along the touchline in joy.

We had some funny moments with Freddie. We were coming back from an away game in London, the club would let them have a few beers on the coach on the way back so we stopped at an off licence near the ground. The owner of the shop must have crapped himself when he saw 17 huge blokes pile into his shop. He was terrified as he was convinced he was about to be robbed. He was smiling though when they left and had purchased most of his stock. It was a happy coach. Halfway back to St Helens, Freddie would get on the mike at the front of the coach and announce, "Right you motherf***ers, we're travelling at 70 miles per hour and I think this f***ing pilot can go faster than that if he puts his f***ing foot down. It's raining outside and if gets his speed up we might manage to land in St Helens and get into Nexus before it shuts". Tuilagi was just like Longy.

Freddie also had very wide feet and his boots would constantly be bursting hence him taking other players boots from time to time. I'd have a go at him over it and he'd just laugh about it. The club shop even sold Freddie wigs. He was very popular with the fans and another big character in the dressing room. You miss people like Freddie.

As a coach, Ellery certainly had good points but I don't think he was the full package. We signed Darrell "Tricky" Trindall at the start of the 2000 season but he didn't last long. He trained well to be fair. Word got through to us that Trindall was leading some of the younger players including Paul Wellens a little bit astray at nights. There were things that had to be sorted out. Fortunately it was sorted out and Wello turned out to be a great player for Saints. As for Trindall, there had been high expectations but nothing materialised.

Ellery left after the first league game of the season at home to Bradford. We didn't know what was going on – players included – although we did know that things weren't right. Ellery had been very outspoken on his views of how the club was run and it did not go down well with the board. When Ellery left the club so did Nigel Ashley-Jones.

17

The Glory Years

We played Bradford in the play offs at the end of 2000 season and as the Bradford fans massed at the Edington end of Knowsley Road near the end of the game, it looked like we had lost. What followed is probably the most replayed rugby league try of all time.

With the "Wide to West" try I'm sure I'm like everyone who was in the stadium that night. It all happened so quickly that I wanted to watch it time and time again. It never really happened for young Westy at Saints but you can never take that moment of history away from him, even if he didn't score the try itself. He came up with the goods with that run. Joynty had Anthony Sullivan screaming for the ball inside him and when asked why he hadn't passed it after the game, Joynty just said: "No bloody chance". It was a fantastic occasion. It was only afterwards I saw the footage of Bradford coach Matthew Elliott disappearing under his seat in the stand.

We ended the 2000 season with Ian Millward in charge and a Grand Final win over Wigan. Always nice to beat the old enemy. Ian had been at Leigh and we had on the board at the time Arthur Thomas who also lived in Leigh who I think was involved in bringing Ian in.

Ian brought some funny things to the club. He came to me one day asking me to make a cone, I got an old traffic cone, sawed the heavy bottom off it leaving it as a dunces hat shape. I drilled two holes through it and put a brush steel through it. It held the ball. As daft as it sounds, Ian then had the players jumping up to try and get the ball.

He also wanted a much higher kicking tee. He figured the lower the tee the less of the ball you can get your foot underneath. He wanted us to have a really high one. We got it made. Give him credit, he was always thinking of things we could do to improve. Whatever he did worked well in those years when you look at the trophies we won during that period. He would say, "We're a unit on the field but we are one off it too. Your kids and your wives, they are part of it too".

Ian was a completely different person to his predecessor Ellery. He was a very friendly, outgoing guy. He wanted to create things for players to do on their downtime. He started having barbecues and having an event where the players could bring their wives and families. There'd be a fancy dress do. That was a great time at the club.

We had a sponsor from Widnes who owned a car business. He hosted an end of season barbecue for players and staff with everything free. All the kids could come and it was a fantastic day out. There were bouncy castles and clowns with balloons. There was a free bar for all the players. He had a nice piece of land with marquees set up on it with food of every description laid on. They had music playing too. It was great. Longy being Longy, there was some comedy. If he gets to my age, he'll still be the same, he'll still be looking on his body for a place to put a tattoo. I love the lad though. We were all sat there with our wives, there was a corn field at this place. Longy said, "I'll see ya". He ran into this corn field and then went down. A few moments later and he popped up like a jack-in-a-box in a different part of the field. This went on for a while and we were all dying laughing at him.

With Ian, we had Jon Sharp, Dave Rotheram and Kieron Purtill. Every morning, I was always first at the club. I would be there at 6.30am. I did everything in those days, sort the kit and wash it. If it was the morning after a very muddy game, I would have to jet wash everything individually before putting kit in the washing machine. The five of us would always have a cup of tea together first thing. It was a chat before starting the day.

From time to time, Ian brought in a psychologist. He would talk to the lads. He talked to us about what was good for a dressing room before a game and what was bad. He said one of the worst things you could see when you walked into a dressing room was the colour purple. He said it was such a depressing colour. Ian then had the idea to paint the away dressing room purple. The psychologist had only spoken to us the day before the game so it transpired that we were still painting it on game day, an hour before the opposition arrived. There were four or five of us at it. Naturally, the away team had a lot to say about it when they arrived.

"What a shit colour this is".

Ian was delighted to hear that as he thought it must be doing the trick. Whether it did or not is a different matter. I remember Shaun McRae bringing Hull there and he asked me who had painted the dressing room like that. He said he didn't care what colour it was. It was all about what his players did out on the pitch.

We later visited Wakefield and they had done their away dressing room the same colour for us, just for that day. I just thought '"well done to them".

2001 and beating Brisbane Broncos in the hailstone at the Reebok Stadium, Bolton for the World Club Championship was one of the best days of my life. We were playing the best team in Australia with Lockyer, Sailor, Tallis, Webcke and so on. We were sat on the benches not far away from the Brisbane bench. They were leading 18-6 and their bench were making sure we knew all about it. I was calling them all the names under the sun under my breath. When we eventually edged in front, you would have thought I had won the lottery. I was really taunting them. What a win. I've had some good moments in my life but that was fantastic.

You can imagine what the dressing room was like afterwards. The lads wanted to exchange shirts because of the win. Some players wouldn't do that; Andy Farrell was one who would never exchange his shirt. He told me that he kept them in a box for his son. I went to the Brisbane dressing room and spoke to Darren Lockyer as the Saints players who wanted to swap wouldn't go themselves. It got sorted.

David Fairleigh had made his Saints debut in that match and was a great player, it's a pity we only had him for twelve months. He was a guy you could always have a bit of fun with. When I started at Saints, there was never bottled water. It was always out of the tap. When I was a kid, not only did I drink it from the tap, I'd drink it out of the streams when I was out playing.

David Fairleigh would always ask me for a bottle of water. It got to the point where I would just reply, "The tap's there".

He would always insist it had to be bottled water as the tap water wasn't right.

"David, we've won two bloody world wars on tap water."

I went onto explain that everyday tap water was tested so it was suitable for drinking.

"Give us a bloody bottle of water! I don't want a lecture."

I made a deal with him that I wouldn't bring the subject up again if he could tell the difference between bottled and tap water. He said he definitely could. I told him I would fill three cups with water and he had to tell me which was the bottled water. He was well up for it. I went into the back room while he stayed in the dressing room and I filled all three cups with tap water. I brought the cups back to the dressing room and told him to tell me which was the bottled water. You would think it was a wine tasting event the way he was carrying on. He was swilling each round his mouth so I shouted, "You can smell them too if you want".

After sipping all three cups, he told me he was undecided but then pointed to a cup and declared that that was the one containing bottled water. I just shook my head.

"Well I wasn't sure," he said. I just told him that the one he had selected was definitely not bottled water and that he should taste the other two again. He tasted them both again and made another guess. I told him again that he was wrong. Alan Clarke was laughing his head off by this point.

"Which is it?" David asked.

"They're all tap water," I replied.

"You little shit," he shouted before proceeding to call me all the names under the sun. I told him that all the bottles he drank out of on match day were all from out of a tap too.

I met up with David when I went over to Australia with Great Britain, and the first thing I said was, "I don't know whether to have a bottle of water. What's your tap water like? It can't be as good as ours".

We beat Bradford at Twickenham in a rainy Challenge Cup Final in 2001 which doesn't really stand out for me looking back. I just don't get the same atmosphere or feeling there that I get at other big grounds.

The 2002 Grand Final against Bradford was another good day for Saints but a bad day for Wello who got took off early with a fractured cheekbone. We won the game with a late Sean Long drop goal before controversy in the dying seconds over an alleged voluntary tackle by Chris Joynt. We got some stick for that. I think it was half and half myself.

Darren Albert had joined the side by this point and was a quiet guy in the dressing room. I appreciated his pace. I used to love the song the Saints fans would sing *Hey Darren Albert* and would often join in whilst sat on the bench. The club did well out of Darren.

We've had some phenomenal matches at Saints in the last couple of decades. If you ask me my standout match of my

121

career in refereeing it would be my last match, the Meninga final. However, the all time highlight would be the 2004 Challenge Cup Final when we beat Wigan in Cardiff. That was my greatest day. They had been selling Longy wigs in the club shop as he had one of his mad hairstyles at the time. I had one in my bag on the bench. We had gradually taken control of that game on the day. It was a red hot day and towards the end of the match, if we scored another try I was going to take the kicking tee on wearing the wig. I was in such a happy mood at beating the auld enemy in a good final. We didn't get a last minute try so I had to be content with running around the pitch with it on after the final hooter. Ian brought that fun culture in. Cardiff was perfect because of the hot weather, the opposition, the way the game went and the characters we had in the team such as Longy. If I'd have gone on the pitch with the kicking tee with a wig on I'd have got in trouble but I can understand how people sometimes do things when they're on an adrenaline high. Half of our supporters got sunburnt that day. At Cardiff our bench was in the sun and some players when being subbed went and stood in the tunnel such was the heat.

Ian Millward left the club in 2005. Whatever happened between Ian and the club, that's their business. My job was my job. Ian wore his heart on his sleeve. I even saw him jump on Longy's back for a piggyback when we'd won a final. Mick Potter was more reserved whilst Royce Simmons was a more serious, thoughtful character

We were successful under Millward and some spectators didn't want him to go. I still have a great relationship with Ian to this day. Celia and I got invited to his wedding. I was sad to see Ian go. We had won so much under him. He married a girl from Leigh and I always got on really well with him.

Kiwi coach Daniel Anderson also fostered a happy culture within the club when he took over the head coach role. He operated a work hard-play hard philosophy. He took us on pre-season training to Marbella one year. It was January so the bars were very quiet there. There was a bar around the corner that the players would go in at night and the owner was glad of the custom. One night Daniel announced that there was to be a Spanish theme to the evening. We had little groups of six people and we had to come down for our evening meal in a Spanish theme. It was great, some players had Mexican hats on, we put moustaches and ponchos on. Star Aussie centre Jamie Lyon's group all just wore a Spanish pinny on the front of them. Daniel joined in with a big sombrero on. Eamonn McManus was there too and was also dressed up. We all piled in the pub. That was a very good night.

We also had a do at the training ground and Maurie Fa'asavalu and some of the other guys dug a pit, then cooked a pig in it. That was great too.

Then for the captains run training session that takes place the day before the match, we had a big barbecue. The injured players got bacon, eggs, sausages, black pudding and toast and served the rest of the players after training. Big winger Francis Meli loved it. That kind of atmosphere suited us more as a club than what we had with Ellery.

Daniel Anderson also brought in an assistant, Harry Bryant. On wet days, we would have a skip full of water. He'd throw all the balls in it then start throwing them to the players to practice handling the balls in very wet conditions. It's all ways of thinking "How do we beat the opposition".

Star player Keiron Cunningham brought in a bloke who had his own gym at Wigan and that's how we got the first proper gym at Knowsley Road. It had been a bar by the main stand and we converted it into a gym. After his playing career, Keiron was another who went into strength and conditioning at Saints.

Things have evolved since then and the gym we have at Cowley is incredible – two level with an oxygen chamber and ice baths.

Ian Millward came back to Saints soon after departing as coach of Wigan who came to play us in the Challenge Cup which Saints won 75-0. I could relate to that though as when I came to Saints with Eric Hughes my first game was against Leigh and we lost. It was a belting score against Wigan but I just felt sorry for Ian.

When we beat Huddersfield at Twickenham in the 2006 Challenge Cup Final. Samoan Maurie Fa'asavalu did a war dance after the game as the trophies kept rolling in.

2006 was the year Saints conquered all. The Grand Final victory was a comfortable win over Hull. Old Trafford is something special; it is a fantastic stadium to host a final. The fans are piled high at Old Trafford; it's akin to the Coliseum. In the dressing room afterwardsthe lads were getting patched up and some were in ice baths but it couldn't stop the celebrations, fun and laughter. Maurie did his war dance again in the dressing room and we belted out our song *Oh when the Saints* which seemed to go on forever on special nights like that one.

Under Daniel Anderson, we went through a spell at finals of pinning photos of each player up in the dressing room over that player's bench. We also took Saints flags to finals. It was so the players weren't walking into too alien a situation. It made them feel more at home seeing the Saints stuff in there.

Daniel Anderson was very regimented in his approach and he was a very good coach. He got upset at me once. Sky came and did a feature on me at home with Eddie Hemmings. It was because I had been involved with the game for such a long time. They then followed me around on my working day at Saints. Then they said they would follow it up by sending a cameraman to follow me around to see what I did on match day. I asked Daniel Anderson would it be ok for them to film me setting up the dressing room. He was quite abrupt but said it would be ok as long as it didn't interfere with the team getting ready. During the game, the cameraman came on the touchline and he was doing shots of me running on the field with the kicking tee. This did not go down well with Daniel. He had a bit of a go at me saying, "We don't want any of that shit again". After that, I did feel that there was a bit of an undercurrent between us. That's the only time I've felt a bit uncomfortable whilst I've been at Saints.

He was an excellent coach though and we had a lot of success under him. He had a very good sidekick with Alan Wilson who was a great assistant. Sometimes I feel that the assistants don't get appreciated for what they do. Kieron Purtill was another one. He really worked hard at the club especially on video work. When the side wins the coach and players get all the credit and not necessarily all the people who help them like the assistant coaches.

Daniel Anderson was very particular about playing kit in that he wanted it to be skin tight. To get them on the players, you near enough needed to oil them into it. Jason Hooper tried his jersey on and wasn't really happy with it. That's what Daniel wanted though. After ten minutes of the game, we more or less had to cut Jason out of it. It was almost choking him. Daniel Anderson called me into his office one day and said that I would no longer be needed full-time, as he was going to give my wage to Ian Harris who was a masseur and he would also do my day duties with the team. My other duties like washing the kit would be passed on to Alan Clarke unpaid.

He then told me I could still help with kit preparation for the team on the captains run and on game day with the dressing room duties and could claim any out of pocket expenses.

I was completely gutted when I left to think that I would no longer be going to work everyday, mixing and having a laugh and a joke with the boys which I had done all my life, first down the mine and now with my mates at the club.

Celia could see what I was like when I came home that day and I lost a few nights of sleep thinking of what I would do now with my days. I do feel the action he took that day was the result of what took place with the Sky feature on me.

But as they say time is a big healer and I have learned to live with it and it has given me more time with Celia and a few more holidays in Lanzarote. Although she has said many a time, "I wish you were at the club and not under my feet".

I had a little cubbyhole room at Knowsley Road at the back. That was my kingdom. I used to tell players that they couldn't go in there without asking me. Freddie Tuilagi was a nightmare for taking anybody's boots. His feet were like two paddles on a steamer – he had very wide, flat feet. So, I had to keep the boot room free from predators. I bought floor tiles for it and did all the work myself. I then painted all the cupboards white. My granddaughter suggested that I get players to sign the cupboards and wall. That's what I did and the players started putting all kinds of comments on there. Jamie Lyon signed it with a comment about his man of steel shirt because he still thinks I took one of his shirts. He reckons I put it on ebay. Nick Fozzard was the artist and would draw pictures of people. All the players signed it, especially when leaving the club. When we left the ground I said that we should have taken those cupboard doors off and brought them to Langtree Park with us.

They filmed the *Best* film at Knowsley Road, the life story of George Best. Ray Wilkins was in that film and he signed my cupboards. Longy put a load of stuff on those cupboards too.

In 2007 we won the World Club Challenge against Brisbane again, another great night. Then we got to the first Challenge Cup Final at the new Wembley in 2007 when we played Catalans. We were all very excited at seeing the new place. Although we found it to be a lovely stadium, there were a lot of things that just weren't as good as the old place. Things like walking through the old tunnel. We were favourites to win the game so the big match nerves weren't quite at the usual level. It isn't just the players who suffer from pre match nerves, the backroom staff do as well. We had to go down before the game to get everything set up just right. It lacked the big bath they had had at the old Wembley and it didn't seem as intimate. . At the new Wembley, they have a bloke in the dressing room who is there to wait on you if you want him to and serve you bottled water.

We went again the year after against Hull, and we knew what to expect then. The game was more of a contest than in 2007 but we still had too much for them. The angriest I have ever seen a Saints coach was Daniel Anderson at half time during the 2008 Grand Final defeat to Leeds. He completely lost it and used every word in the book. I had seen it in the past from the likes of Alex Murphy, Frankie Barrow, Kevin Ashcroft and Maurice Bamford but it was out of the ordinary for a modern day coach. Looking at the lads faces I don't think some of the things he said went down too well. After the game, he apologised.

Mick Potter took over from Daniel and was a very quiet guy but a nice person to work with. We did have one thing in common though as he had worked in the mining industry in Australia. I believe since finishing playing Jason Hooper has gone into mining over there.

St Helens leaving Knowsley Road was sad but inevitable. The ground was steeped in history. The stories that came out of the place were unbelievable. When we knew we had to leave, there was understandably a lot of nostalgia. We'd been leaving eight years previously in the Mally Kay era so we'd seen plans before but this was different. The place had become really tired – the drains at the scoreboard end of the ground under the pitch had collapsed so it was really boggy. It became really heavy there and it was a big job for the groundsman to sort. The corrugation roof of the stand was blowing off in winter. The electrics were shot. We had problems with the plumbing in the old dressing room – we still had lead piping there! I know that sounds like something from Cluedo and with the water coming through those old pipes, maybe David Fairleigh had a point after all. We had break in's at the ground where the windows were smashed and all the kit was pinched. In reality we were all looking forward to moving but the spectators still loved the atmosphere at Knowsley Road. And don't get me wrong, once the players got out onto that pitch, they forgot everything bad behind the scenes.

We had a year at Widnes in 2011 whilst in transition and it was a poor year. First of all we were down 2,000 supporters with every gate. They just weren't travelling. I asked one man and he said he had two kids and he would have had to have got a bus to Widnes whereas he just used to walk to Knowsley Road but hardest hit were the Knowsley Road chippies. Every home match at Widnes was an away match for us really. We didn't have a room to store kit in so had to transport it to and from every game. The atmosphere in the dressing room wasn't the same either. You knew you were walking into the home dressing room of Widnes. They had a couple of club signs up in there which we covered up on match days. It wasn't our own. Even the stewards were different to the ones at Knowsley Road who we had got to know so well.

With any coach, you try to engage them in conversation at some point. Royce Simmons, who replaced Mick Potter, was the hardest bloke ever to have a conversation with. Sometimes at Widnes, there would only be me, Alan Clarke and Royce in the dressing room and he wouldn't say a word. It was very uncomfortable at times. I remember the coach trip to Cardiff for the Magic Weekend and he never spoke to us. Alan Clarke and myself felt completely out of it.

Scrum half Kyle Eastmond was a mummy's lad I think. He comes from Oldham and having refereed there I would joke with him in the middle of July about them still having snow there. I could always have a chat and a laugh with him. He was going to be the next Sean Long, a position the club had groomed him for. He had come through the system. He did seem to pick up a few injuries. He was a pleasant lad although on match days he showed a bit of petulance at times when things weren't just going right. One occasion was Keiron Cunningham's last match. Kyle wasn't on the pitch and had gone into the dressing room sulking. Like all the young players, he was always on his mobile phone. I don't know how I managed without a phone when I was a young lad. I once asked him if he ever voted. He told me he wasn't bothered who got in. I explained to him that I was coming to the end of my life and he should be looking for what was good for the country. I told him it was down to him and others of his generation to help shape the country's future. We then started talking about the conflict in Afghanistan and he said he wouldn't go to war. I told him he would if someone invaded and came through his front door. He insisted that he wouldn't but I told him he would protect his own home. I said there was so much going on in the world with bombings and with the Twin Towers on 9/11 but he was having none of it.

Kyle moved to rugby union with Bath at the end of 2011. I still exchange the odd text with him. It's a shame for the club though because we are still feeling the legacy of letting Matty Smith go to keep Eastmond who then left. It's meant we have been at least a half back short for a number of seasons. It backfired on us.

Between 2007 and 2011 we did of course lose five Grand Finals in a row. So disappointing. They always say it's hard losing in a semi final but losing in a final is worse. The disappointment is very hard to take. That's why you see players crying on the pitch. It really gets to them. They stay on the pitch to go and collect their medals. In reality they'd prefer to get off that pitch as quickly as possible. They just want to get back to the dressing room while the winners celebrate.

So often we've been the ones celebrating, but to lose then lose again the following year is soul destroying. It got to the third year and I said to Alan Clarke, "If we lose this one and come back next year, I'm not coming". You don't mean it of course but that's how it makes you feel. I love Grand Final night and Manchester United's ground but we've had a lot of disappointments there. We've had United's dressing room and the away dressing room, that's not made a difference.

It would be lovely to go back there and end the night singing that song of ours in the winning dressing room. Everybody connected with the club shares that desire. I look back at little incidents during those five finals: wet conditions with Sinfield's kicking causing us problems. Rob Burrows' try where he ran at Scott Moore to go through – that broke my heart. He did the business, such a dangerous player, ducking under tackles.

The last time Saints reached the Grand Final was in 2011. My grandson Garry carried the Super League trophy out before the game in his RAF uniform, a very proud moment for the whole family. He's a Wigan fan sadly, as is my daughter Sharon and her husband Kevin which is where Garry has got it from.

Mike Rush, our chief executive, has set up a terrific youth system for the club. He has his own team of men who are around him and they are bringing the youth through. Alongside Keiron Cunningham he stood in as head coach when we were without one for the bulk of the 2012 season and between them they did quite a good job. Now, he has an even bigger job.

18

Characters at Saints

There are so many funny moments from throughout my time at Saints involving many different players. One player we had great humour with was Paul Newlove. When he first came to Saints, I remember asking him, "How have Bradford got on?"

"I don't know," he'd reply, "I haven't got Sky".

He wasn't interested in rugby apart from playing. It was a living for him. A lot of people are like that in that they go to work and don't necessarily love it.

He had a few hens scratching about on his property on a small holding. He had had problems with rats on his smallholding as well as with foxes trying to get his hens. Keiron Cunningham suggested to Newy that with the fox coming regularly, he should tie a chicken to a tree and be standing by with a gun. Newy is the last person I'd give a gun to personally. Newy then went in with a farmer for some cows but Foot and Mouth disease then struck which caused him all kinds of problems. No sympathy for him in the dressing room though as players shouted that they didn't want him to come near them with his disease.

After training at Knowsley Road, the players would go for lunch in the restaurant. We got a bowl, filled it with water and mixed some soap suds in it. We made a big notice that we put up saying 'everybody is allowed in the restaurant except Paul Newlove and owing to the foot and mouth outbreak, he must remove his shoes and socks to wash his feet in this bowl of disinfectant.

He came up and said, "I'm not doing that". Eventually, he took his shoes and socks off and had a quick dip.

We went on a pre-season training camp to Marbella. The season before, Paul had snapped his Achilles which in years gone by was a career ending injury. Paul couldn't train at the time of the trip but we took him as well. He was in rehab and Claire Mannion was the physio at the time. She had to set something for Paul to do every day. We went to the training pitch and she started putting different coloured cones down in a circuit. She wanted him to jog round them. He looked at the circuit and said, "All round the bloody pitch?"

"Yes," she said.

"If I'd have known I had to do all this, I'd have brought my bloody dog."

One day, she took him to the beach and for something different made him get into a boat with the instruction, "As long as you don't go too far out of sight you'll be ok".

Another time, we were playing London and we had travelled down the day before. We'd arrive around teatime and we would have a training session. This occasion, Ian Millward said training would be between 6.30pm and 7.30pm. Newy started shaking his head and said, "We can't train tonight".

"Why?" asked Millward.

"Don't you realise Jack could lose his farm tonight?"

"What?"

"Jack Sudgen is in court tonight and could lose his farm. It's Emmerdale tonight."

The day after, Newy came down to breakfast beaming, "It's alright, he got off".

They always said Newy was frightened of flying, which was a wrong. What he was frightened of was things like going through an airport on his own, dealing with passport control and so on. When Saints went out to Australia for the 1997 World Club Challenge, he missed his flight. We had to send a kid from the Academy, Jason Johnson, to fly with Newy. Jason loved this as he had no playing responsibilities so had the holiday of a lifetime.

Another time we were over there and we stopped off in Hong Kong. I was sat with Newy and Joynty as I would often do as they were good fun to be around. The two of them would always bunk in together wherever they travelled. Joynty would always say, "Newy's got to find his first penny," as he would never spend any money. Joynty told Newy to go and get him some food. He told Newy what he wanted from the Chinese style restaurant and I picked mine. Newy panicking said, "Stan, come with me". He wouldn't go and order the food on his own. Coming back on that trip we flew into London. Instead of him getting the flight back to Manchester with the rest of us, Howesy had arranged for him to fly back to Yorkshire. When he did that, somebody had to go with him to show him where to check in.

I have an apartment in Lanzarote now but before we had it, my friend had it. Newy asked him about it and decided to spend a week there with his wife and two kids. My friend gave Newy detailed instructions on how to get to the apartment from the airport. Naturally Newy lost the directions and only knew the name of the town it was in. Fortunately my friend went looking for him and found him on the pavement with his family and suitcases.

Another time training at La Santa in Lanzarote and thanks to Newy's broken clock, Ian Millward fined him and Chris Joynt for being late for a training session. The money went into a beer kitty for the players at the end of the trip. There was a sports bar on the complex for a few drinks. Guess who were the first two in the bar? Newy and Joynty with the former exclaiming, "I'm having my moneys worth".

The next day, the players were given a free afternoon. With me knowing Lanzarote a bit, Newy and Joynty asked where was best to go. There was me, Ian Millward, his assistant Harry Bryant, Newy and Joynty who went off together. We found a couple of little bars a couple of miles away from the camp and had a good afternoon. I'm not a good drinker and soon had enough so I made my way back leaving them to it. They stopped there and I found out later they had started ordering pizzas into the bar.

I think I could do a book on Newy alone. He had to travel from Pontefract but he was always first to training. He always wanted to be first away as well. One day Ian Millward spoke to Joynty just after a session had finished saying he wanted all the players for a team meeting. Joynty said, "Newy will be at the service station on the motorway by now". Newy once said, "I come all the way from Pontefract and every day all we do is train". "That's your job," I would tell him. I don't know if he was expecting some nice days out.

I organised our nights out when Saints went to Lanzarote with Ian Millward. There's an old town at Porta Del Carmen and they have a big Chinese restaurant. Whenever we book, we always tell the restaurant that we have guys coming in who could eat the table top. We also have to tell them that the players don't like waiting. They sit down and think that the food should be put in front of them immediately. What we do is if we go to an Italian, we tell them to put fifteen pizzas along the table as soon as they get there. Whilst they're eating those pizzas, we ask the waiters to come in and take their orders. So, before we got to the Chinese, we told them to put some soup on and some chicken wings. We were after a banquet type meal. As the meal went on the lady who owned the restaurant brought around free drinks for everybody which is a custom over there. She could see we were all having a good time, she had a towel wrapped round a bottle. She asked Newy would he like a drink. He eyed her suspiciously and asked what it was. She said it was an aperitif. I said he should have a go as it would probably be good for his sex life. She filled his glass and he emptied it.

"That's shite," he said proving a job as a food critic would always be beyond him.

She took the towel away and there was a lizard in the bottle.

When Saints played at Castleford in 2013, I bumped into Newy at the game. It is always good to see him because he was something else at Saints. A mate of Newy's came looking for me before the game and led me to a beer tent where he was having a pint on a very hot day. His mate started mithering me for a t-shirt which I explained I couldn't give him. Newy had a nice shirt on with a pair of shorts. I looked at his shorts and realised they were a pair from 1996 with an old faded Saints logo on.

"Newy, surely you could get a new pair of shorts?"

"They still fit". After the game, we went for some food and Newy was there again. We were having a good chinwag about old times. My mate Alan Clarke was there and he reminded me of the time we went to London with Saints. After breakfast, there would always be time to have a little walk around so me, Alan, Joynty and Newy decided to go for a stroll. We ended up down some rather dodgy side streets with vagrants asleep in them. Joynty said to Newy, "That could be us that Newy, go and see if he's alright".

"I'm not waking him up Joynty, he might want 50p".

I always got on well with Joynty. We would take the Michael out of each other a bit. He would always have a lot to say. On pre-season training when we had free time, he would always grab me and Newy to go for a walk. One time in Porta Banus, we went to a bar for a couple of beers to watch the world go by. The harbour was a millionaire's playground and it was interesting people watching.

Joynty has a really dry sense of humour. We'd get free t-shirts from companies from time to time and I would give them to the players to train in. I'd tell Joynty I had free stuff and he'd say, "If it's free bring a wheelbarrow". That was one of his favourite sayings.

At Knowsley Road, there was the home and away dressing rooms. At training, the first team players would use the home dressing room and the younger players would change in the away dressing room. Eric Ashton was chairman and insisted that the first team players should use that home dressing room. He felt that once you made it into there you had made your name. Joynty never would though, he'd always use that away room as would Newy. With Joynty and Newy in the Ateam dressing room, Apollo Perelini decided to join them. Apollo used to take towels home with him from the club. Someone reckoned he must have had about 10 Saints towels there on his washing line.

At half time during matches, the coach would always have his say but so would Joynty. "We're letting them up too soon to play the ball, we've got to hold them down longer," he would always tell them. The second half would start and the first three penalties would be against Joynty for holding down. Jon Wilkin is like that today.

Joynty was a great guy. He was the ultimate professional. Him and Tommy Martyn were the last of the players who had a job outside of rugby when they signed for Saints. Joynty would be getting up at half past four in the morning delivering milk. The players today don't have any concept of what that must be like and I worry about some of them with what they'll do after their rugby career is over. Alex Murphy often says what type of player he would have been had he been a full-time professional. Once Joynty has made his mind up about something, that's it, he doesn't vary from it. What a great captain.

Steve Prescott had no meat on him, just like myself. When he first started coming through at Saints, I had memories of his dad, Eric, who I had refereed on numerous occasions. They were two different types of players though from very different eras. Eric was a hard case. Steve didn't quite have the same stature as his dad. He wasn't as big but he scored some fantastic tries. He had such pace. His defensive play was strong too. When he went to Hull, I was sorry to see him go. I thought he had given us so much. He didn't want to go but he went and he was successful. I would always catch up with him when Saints played against Hull. Simon Booth, a Leyther, went to Hull at that time from Saints too.

Steve made a good name for himself, both at St Helens and at Hull. The spectators at both clubs loved him. It's so sad that Steve succumbed to his illness in November 2013. A great lad and a good player. What he did for charity throughout his illness is nothing short of inspirational. His legacy of courage and inspiration will endure.

Tommy Martyn was a Leigh lad who came to Saints from Oldham. He was a good player, another chatty bloke. He might have lacked a yard of pace but overall he was fantastic. He was also a good kicker. I think he had a little bit of bad feeling in regards to how much Australian players got paid at Saints. They would come over and have a house sorted for them with all fixtures and fittings. Tommy was someone who had previously had to work full-time, as a wagon driver. He had to get up early in the morning to work and then play his rugby as well.

Barry Ward came to Saints and he was a big lad, he was a bit overweight. Barry had come over with Darren Britt who was a fabulous bloke. Wardy was on the jolly side and it seemed that Tommy Martyn had introduced him to the delights of the Crispy Cod. Wardy was made up with having mushy peas on his chips. The club ended up asking the chippy to ban him from being served there anymore.

Wardy turned up at the club one day in a fantastic sponsored car and it obviously hit a raw nerve with Tommy. It was like the valve going on a pressure cooker. "These bloody Aussies, where the bloody hell has he got that from?"

Tommy had a knack for interceptions. He could mind read what players were going to do. One of his best was at Wigan when we beat the pie eaters after trailing all game.

I was jumping off the bench when he did that, especially because it was against them. I pay my tax to Wigan now much to my annoyance. I had refereed Tommy's dad and had never got on with him. His dad was a rough character but he could play too and had a skilful offload. I played with his uncle Mickey. He was a belting second rower and could score some tries. They are a real rugby family and I know his son is coming through the ranks now.

Keiron Cunningham was just one of the guys who came to the club and went about his job without bothering anybody. He's a deep thinker and knew what he had to do. He would always give you one hundred per cent every match he played. He didn't need a lot of motivation to go out and get on with the job. What a great, great player. He came through the system at Saints and gave everything for the club. I get on really well with Keiron. He changed his lifestyle part way through his career. He doesn't drink any alcohol and is a real family man. I chat to him quite a bit and he always asks after Celia. How much pleasure has he given the people of St Helens? He was a special player and totally dedicated – a good, hard player but never dirty.

Kevin Iro was a bit straight laced, but he was a gentleman. I was a bit in awe of him when he came to the club. He was a great player for us. Sadly towards the end we had to nurse him from game to game due to a leg problem. I'd sometimes work out in the gym at the same time as him. I'd be on the rowing machine at the side of him, albeit not going the same speed as him. One day, he'd been on it so long I asked him, "Is there any land in sight?"

When you look back at the centres we've had at Saints from Meninga to Iro to Newlove to Lyon to Gidley, it's incredible really.

I had the closest relationship with Longy and often when he'd successfully converted a try he wouldpat me on the head after the kick. It was almost a father-son relationship. That was picked up by fans of other clubs, I remember one

Wakefield lady saying, "Are you sure you're not related to Longy?"

There would be times he would see me and him on the big screen and he'd do the bunny ears with his fingers on top of my head. How many times did Longy win us a game with a drop goal? Certainly the 2004 Grand Final win against Bradford comes to mind as does a last gasp winner at Knowsley Road against Warrington.

Longy was a one off. David Howes brought him to the club from Widnes. They haggled on the deal from early in the morning to late in the afternoon. The word eventually came through that we had got him. What a good signing he was. Him and Tommy struck up such a good relationship at half back. Never in a million years did I think I would strike up such a good friendship with him. It's probably the best relationship in all my career I've had with a player. I did see myself in him. He made me a public figure with some of the things he did when I brought on his kicking tee in televised games. It even gave me a bit of a fan club at Wakefield with a group of women there. It even got to the point where I'd be on holiday having a meal with Celia in a restaurant and people would come up to me saying, "I know you, you're that bloke who takes the kicking tee on for Longy".

I've not read a lot of player's books but it does make me laugh towards the end of Longy's book where he says that his next book will be about rugby. His book was all about his life and was extremely funny. I was involved in a lot of the things that he put in his book.

We were training in Marbella one pre-season and there was a Russian football team also over there at the same time. They were in the same hotel as us. In our spare time, we were allowed to wear our own leisure kit. They always had to wear the club gear which generally was a plain tracksuit. They would walk past us in the corridor, always with long faces. By contrast, our lads were always bubbly and smiling.

We'd get to our rugby training pitch and the football

training pitch would be right at the side of it. There was very little interaction with any of the Russians. We had finished our ball play and one or two of our lads were just watching what the Russians were doing in training. Suddenly, a near naked Longy ran on their pitch, side stepped one or two of them, jumped up and did ten chin ups on the crossbar. We were all in floods of laughter. The Russians were all very straight faced at his antics probably thinking "crazy English man". It was always off the cuff stuff with Longy.

When Longy left Saints to go to Hull it felt like I'd lost my right arm. We played Hull that year and before the game one of their directors said to me, "I thought you'd have come up here with him". I really missed him. We still have a good relationship but I've not gone as far as to have tattoos like him.

Jamie Lyon was a brilliant player. During breaks in training, the players would sometimes play cricket and it would end up Australia v England. There would be a lot of rivalry if it coincided with the real Ashes. Wello would always be involved, and got stuck in even if they only had tennis balls to play with.

Jamie and I would always have a lot of banter. He came to me one day wrestling me, when I turned my back and threw him down to the ground. "You little sod," he said.

Paul Sculthorpe came to us from Warrington. He turned out to be one of the best things to ever happen to Saints. Scully and I really hit it off straightaway.

Brian Noble would always say in international camp, "If you want anything don't come to me, go to Stan. If he can't sort it out, you can come to me". Players would always be mithering for things. Wello is murder for never bringing his underpants with him for match days. It's got to the point that I have a box of underpants at the club especially for him. I could have stocked out the undies section at Marks and Spencers with what I've given him over the years. Scully was like that albeit not as bad.

Scully would always want to clip me and have a bit of a wrestle with me. You have to admire everything he achieved in his career. It was lovely for me to be involved with a character like that. To this day, we have a really good relationship. There was one final we had won and as we were doing the lap of honour I saw a box on the floor. It was one of our lads winners medal. I put it in my pocket. In the dressing room I announced, "We're well off today, I've got a medal". I asked if any of the players if they were missing theirs and it was Scully's. He was delighted to get it. He is a champion fella. He was no trouble whatsoever and was a very good captain.

Matt Gidley was just a nice person. I was ready for him coming to the club as Brian Carney had played alongside him at Newcastle Knights. I had a good relationship with Brian through Great Britain. Brian had told Matt that I would look after him. Matt knew all about me before he met me. Just before he arrived I got a phone call, "Hi, I'm Matt Gidley, a friend of Brian Carney. I believe you can get me some boots sorted out."

"Yeah, no problems." Turns out it was bloody Carney. I fell for it hook, line and sinker. Matt was a great fella though. He followed in the footsteps of Jamie Lyon who was another fantastic person. With Jamie, he'd been used to the Australian system of players looking after all their own boots. He was surprised that this was done for the players in England. They loved it.

One set of Yorkshire lads who came to Saints were a complete crazy gang; Nick Fozzard, Leon Pryce and Lee Gilmour. Fozzard was the craziest of the three. What a trio that was. They'd be the last to arrive at training, and led by Fozzard, they would come in clapping and chanting, "Yorkshire, Yorkshire, Yorkshire". They came to me one day asking me for a signed shirt and they weren't bothered what condition the shirt was in.

"You're not having one," I said.

"How about an old training ball then?"

"What's going on here?"

"Well, on way home from training we always call in at the McDonalds on the Linkroad and a girl who works there is a Saints fanatic. She's told us if we bring her some signed merchandise we are on for free breakfast every day". I did fix them up with something.

Nick Fozzard was a great lad and the last of the funny breed as I call him. The officials are meant to check the players strapping before a game but Nick Fozzard looked as if he had a false leg strapped to his arm. He could have hid anything under that. He didn't do by the way.

I still keep in touch with Foz. The day before one trip to play Londonme, Foz and Alan Clarke went and had a coffee. Foz confided in us that he was nearing the end of his career and didn't have an idea of what he would do with himself once his playing days were over as he had no qualifications. Players never dream about the moment it all ends. We decided we would go through different things we felt he could do. The list was something like this: lollipop man, bin man, dog walker. We were having a good laugh. I was totally surprised when he ended up working in business development on the commercial side of the game, first at Castleford, then at Wakefield. He would always sign his Christmas cards with him, his wife and Molly, his dog. He'd even put a paw print on the card. Fozz was a real nitwit. In the current squad, we've got Louis McCarthy Scarsbrook who is very loud.

There were no players I didn't get on with, even the ones that were awkward such as Prycey. Leon was a good player; he gave me and Allan Clarke headaches though with his kit. The players would have kit ordered for them in the pre-season, but whatever size kit Leon had asked for, when it arrived he would ask for a different size. On a match day you'd get his boots out that he'd brought himself. Before kick off, he'd generally ask you to change his studs, which I'd do for him. He'd warm up for about two minutes before he'd send word in that he wanted different studs again. There's eight studs on a boot so that's sixteen studs to change in about three minutes. This would happen week in week out. When Leon left for Catalans, I wondered how the French kitman would get on with him.

Gilly would be the same with changing shorts and when he asked me I would always say, "Gilly, you are one Yorkshire pillock".

Foz would come up later in the day and say, "Tell Gilly what he is," and I'd repeat it. It would become a bit of a punch line that phrase.

When Mickey Higham joined Saints from Leigh I found him to be a terrific lad. What you see in Micky's play is what you get with him off the field as well – tonnes of enthusiasm and a great trainer. I think he realised when he joined the club that he wasn't at the very top level but he wanted to get there and trained forever to ensure he did. He comes from West Leigh and we'd need another book to understand his dialect. Mind you, when Andy Haigh was at Saints he couldn't understand what I was saying. It was nice to see Mickey break into the Saints team. He would do anything for you. Not so long ago, I asked him to go to a school near mine to give out some presentations and he did it. He had attended that school himself. I'm really pleased at how well he has developed his game at Warrington. Every time he sees me when Warrington come to Saints, it's not just a handshake with him, he always gives me a big hug. He actually played with my grandson Gary who now plays for the Combined Services RL team.

Willie Talau could be a handful. He was a really good player but an awkward person off the pitch. Every week, we would get requests from supporters or the club to get players to sign shirts. I'd go round the dressing room after training to get the players to all sign these items. Every time I went to Willie, he'd say, "I'm not signing it".

It got to the point where I would walk past Willie and ask the player next to him. He'd then say, "Are you not asking me?"

"No," I'd reply. "I'm not particularly bothered whether you sign it or not."

That tactic sometimes worked on him as occasionally he'd sign it. Then there'd be times where he would want a ball signing for someone. He'd ask me to get it signed and I would always say, "No". Sometimes items would come down from the Boardroom to be signed, Willie would refuse to sign it and I would say, "It's alright, I'll just tell the chairman that Willie Talau has refused to sign it". That was the way I had to try and get through to him.

Sean Hoppe was a terrific guy, what a personality. He was a true gent and a good player. He would play anywhere in the backs for you. I'd be carrying tackle shields out onto the training pitch and he would always give me a hand. That would happen every time both going on the pitch and coming back off it. Players today will just walk past me when I'm carrying stuff and I have a little joke with them asking them who will win the Sean Hoppe trophy at the end of the season. They ask what it is and I tell them, "It's for the guy who says, 'Stan can I give you a hand?'"

James Graham – like they say about people with red hair – could be short tempered. As a young lad breaking through, we didn't know what we were getting but we soon found out what we had and now know what we miss. If we were losing, he could get into tantrums. After one Grand Final victory, James fell asleep after a few drinks so Leon Pryce sprayed his hair black. When James woke up, he was a raging bull. There was a bit of an altercation between him and Leon. What a player James was.

My outstanding memory of Paul Anderson was his touchline conversion against Leeds at Knowsley Road. He was never a problem in the dressing room. It's nice to see people like Paul doing well in the game as a coach now.

Same with Keiron Purtill who I have a lot of time for. He's a tremendous worker, so enthusiastic and with attention to detail. It seems like the Huddersfield players are playing for the two coaches.

Francis Meli was very dry in the dressing room. He wasn't playing one game and came up to me when I was getting everything ready and asked me if I could get him a turkey butty.

"Who do you think I am, Tesco?" I told him. "No I can't."

When he asked for a turkey butty at Magic Weekend, I did ask him would a jaffa cake do. That's the way Franny was. He did some very unusual things. At half time, he would lie on the dressing room floor stretching whilst Nathan Brown was giving his team talk. Franny would sometimes just point to a pair of shorts that he had without speaking. I generally just pointed back at him or asked him if it was a guessing game.

"Too big," he would murmur quietly.

"You asked for XL," I would protest.

"Too big," he would insist.

I would then give him an L to wear and think that is him sorted.

The next week, he would point again and say, "Too small".

We always have drinks ready to give the players at half time such as water and Powerade, and again Franny would point at the bottles without speaking.

"What do you want?"

"Water," would finally come the response.

We were at training one day and it was raining. Alan Clarke came in the dressing room laughing with a message from Meli saying I had to go and get him a new wet top from the club shop.

"Tell him to sod off," I replied.

He was always the last to get showered and changed after a game too. I would be sat round waiting for ages for his shirt, shorts and socks. I eventually got them. He was sat cleaning his boots with a white towel after one match. I said, "Franny, you don't clean your boots with a white towel. What would your wife say if she saw you doing that?"

"It's in my contract that I can clean my boots with a white towel," was his droll reply.

There wasn't much I could say to that apart from "Ok, I'll tell the woman who washes it". He has a very dry sense of humour.

Today's players do make me laugh at times. You would think they were going to a wedding rather than playing rugby. We have the players sizes written down so when I get the 17 each week, I look down the list and get them the appropriate kit. I put this kit out in the dressing room ready. Francis Meli takes XL shorts but he would go in the dressing room first and try Lance Hohaia's on instead. Lance then would go in saying he has XL shorts. Franny could be a pain in the backside like that at times.

I've had players come to me who wear XL saying the shorts don't fit right and could they try an L. I take the shorts out, rip the label out, give them back to the player who puts them on and says, "They're much better". I put it down to nerves; Paul Clough is a bit like that.

Wello is a gentleman. He's turned into a good captain and he's coming to the end now as happens to all players. He speaks well in the dressing room. I know he finds it very hard watching from the bench and you can see him making every tackle whilst sat there. He wants to be amongst it.

In the old dressing room at Knowsley Road, Mark Edmondson would often be found stood on the bench to look at himself in the mirror before going out to play. He would ask me, "Do my shorts look alright, Stan?"

"They are for working in," I would tell him.

Look at Jamie Foster today. One game he was tackled three times early on and didn't have a hair out of place. I reckon he gelled his hair with cement.

I always had to take three inches off Brian Carney's Great Britain shirt to make it shorter for him. With Jamie Foster, he took his shirt home for his mum to alter it so it hugged his hips.

19

International Camps

David Howes was steeped in the game of rugby league and was very knowledgeable. Because of this he was appointed team manager for Great Britain and England. He brought me in as equipment manager for the international set up.

I started under the then England coach, John Kear. I did exactly what I did for Saints there, sorting out what size kit each player would need. Prior to the 2000 World Cup, David Howes told us that we would be going away on a training camp in Orlando USA.

We got there and the complex was fantastic. David Waite was part of John's backroom staff and I roomed with David. The room was sensational. It came complete with a Jacuzzi.

We trained at Walt Disney's Wild World of Sport. We trained there every day and the facilities were fantastic. Pitch side they had a couple of glamour girls in tight shorts bringing us buckets of ice. They were waiting on us hand and foot even though many of the players were a bit distracted by them.

We would do training and ball work then one night we went for dinner at Epcot. Inside they have different areas for different countries so there's a Canadian section and so on. We went to an Italian restaurant in the "Little Italy" section. The meal was exceptionally good. We then went to the England section and there was a pub called the "Rose and Crown" which we took over for the night. It wasn't about drinking though, and we went into the gardens which were on the edge of a huge lake. We then watched the best firework display I have ever seen. It was a fantastic night.

While over there we went to watch baseball and we played a nine hole golf tournament. Everything was planned. We went to one of the theme parks and one of the rides was called "The Tower of Terror". Inside it was like a church to start with. You sat in a pew then the pews all started moving. Mike Forshaw was very nervous and knew I had been to Orlando before with my family. He said, "What's this Stan?"

"It's not so bad," I lied having been on the ride before.

As the ride continued we went into a lift which took off like a moon rocket. The lift was in complete darkness and zooming up sending your stomach all over the place. When it stops, the door opens and you're overlooking the whole of Orlando. The doors then shut and you rocket straight back down. Mike Forshaw was by this point screaming his head off. We got off the ride and he called me all the names under the sun.

By the side of that ride was another rollercoaster called "Rock N Roll". Now I I generally avoid things like that. However, being with a gang of lads, there was no other alternative. We finished the ride and the guy running it said, "Do you want to go around again lads?"

All the happy shouts of "Yeah" were drowned out my insistent "No". I didn't feel too good when I got off that.

The last day whilst the lads were having the training session, David Howes grabbed me and said we needed find somewhere to get something to eat for the lads later. He told me he had heard of a bar he thought the lads might enjoy called "Hooters". All the waitresses there had big boobs in tight tops so I agreed with him that this would go down well with the lads. We took the lads and they were delighted as there was barbecued chicken for them to get stuck into but I think they probably enjoyed the sight of the waitresses

149

more. It finished the trip on a high note.

England's World Cup campaign was to be launched at the home of rugby union, Twickenham, against Australia. The day of the game was a really soggy affair. It never stopped raining and I don't like Twickenham personally anyway. Unfortunately we didn't start too well as Australia went on to win the game 22-20

England's performances, much like the tournament itself, didn't catch fire and we went out after a very disappointing performance in the semi final against New Zealand.

There was some negativity surrounding David Waite when he took the Great Britain job in 2001, simply because he was Australian. I got on with him really well from the start though. He had a very good knowledge of the game. Since his GB days, he has always treated me very well. I catch up with him these days when Saints play Catalans.

Before the 2001 Ashes series against Australia a motivational company came in and were telling us how to motivate ourselves and how to motivate the team. That was a fabulous night, one of the best nights we've had. The speaker got the group to motivate one another. He had them breaking boards with their fists. He paired people up who were similar in size so one could hold the board while the other broke it. I was paired with David Waite. You could hear players yelling, "I'm going to smash that board".

"No you won't," would come the equally as fierce reply.

In a lot of cases they did it, just through sheer motivation. I was yelling at David, "Come on you big soft so and so," to motivate him. That was what Alex Murphy used to do. That's how he worked in the dressing room. He used to motivate players by, calling them and bullying them.

At the start of the session the speaker lit a huge fire outside, about 15 metres long, all made from wood. He took us outside at the start of the night to look at it whilst it was all flaming. He told us that at the end of the night we were all going to run through it. The players were shaking their heads and muttering, "No chance".

He told us that when preparing for any big game, you could motivate yourself but with the help of somebody else you can motivate one another to push your boundaries further than you previously could.

At the end of the night, he took us out and this fire had died down. It was just red ash all the way along. He'd asked us to all pick a word of our own, just like when you're jumping out of a plane you might yell "Geronimo". It was all about getting worked up and when you were frightened, saying your word. We were all in our bare feet and Paul Anderson was in front of me saying, "I'm not going through that me".

"You big soft sod," I said to him, "if I can do it, you can do it". That's motivation. With Baloo, as Paul Anderson is known, underneath that big exterior he has a really friendly smile. He is a gentle giant off the field. When we ran across the hot coals, we had to pick a word or phrase to shout out, some used Geronimo, I think Paul's was "holy shit".

We all ended up going through it. There was a bucket of water at the other end if you wanted to put your feet in it. It was overcoming fear. That's one of the best things I've done.

In 2001, we surprised everybody by beating Australia in the first Ashes test at Huddersfield but unfortunately we lost the next two. The players had worked really hard going to La Santa under David Waite for warm weather training. Winning that test against the Aussies had me jumping out of my seat. I felt part of it and the doctor, Chris Brookes, was the same.

In 2002, we had a one off July test match in Sydney. It resulted in an embarrassing 64-10 record defeat for Great Britain. We only went over for a week; with the jet lag when I got home I didn't know what day it was. We had very little time to acclimatise. They battered us. The Aussies are very hard people and they made a joke out of it with Andrew Johns being quoted as saying that he didn't need a shower after the game because he hadn't got dirty. That's why I was made up before the 2008 World Cup when Leon Pryce said he'd rather have Blackpool than Bondi. The Aussies don't like things like that. The night before the game we had been invited to a function where some of their former great players were up on a stage talking about the game. We nearly walked out due to the lack of respect we were shown. I wish I could sleep on a plane like some of the players can. We were all just glad to get home. That was the biggest disappointment I endured whilst part of the international set up.

When we climbed Sydney Harbour Bridge in 2002, Paul King the Hull prop wouldn't do it. Scully didn't want to do it either but did it after I called him a big soft so and so. It was a great experience. We all had to be breathalysed before going on. We were then suited up and up we went.

We ended that year in a three match test series at home to New Zealand.

In November 2003, the Aussies came over for three test matches. We lost all three but in each case lost the match in the last five minutes. The first one was 22-18, the second one was 23-20 and the third one was 18-12. It was just the class acts in the Aussie side that got them home. They've always had them, the likes of Meninga, Sterling and this time it was Darren Lockyer. When they got their late tries, if there had been a hole there I would have jumped in it. In the first test, we were down to 12 men within the first few seconds after Adrian Morley was sent off for the first tackle of the game. He copped Robbie Kearns a pearler. I went into the dressing room to see Adrian. There was just me and him sat there for a while. He just had his head in his hands.

They were good matches to be involved in. There had been a great build up and the coaching staff had worked really hard. Spectators say, "When are we going to win a series?" and the coaches are asking exactly the same question. Each time, we think we are going to finally do it. The thing is it's the national game in Australia. I watch the NRL and some of it is brutal. The NRL is a whole other level above Super League.

In the 2004 Tri Nations we made the final but were once again taken apart by Australia in a one sided Elland Road final. I don't really like that ground. For a big club like Leeds United, the dressing rooms are poor. After the game, the players were just sat around in silence. They were reliving the game, wondering where it had gone wrong. The coaches had their work cut out trying to pick the players up.

The 2005 Tri Nations series had its own DVD documentary made: *A League of Their Own*. We went to Marbella to prepare which involved team bonding activities including us all having a go at kayaking on the sea. Each team had to paddle the kayak round a buoy and then back to the shore and then the next man would jump in. It was a huge laugh. Getting away from the side was hard enough because of the waves coming in. Brooksy was on one of the teams. He is a great character, a fitness fanatic but has no co-ordination. Then there was a beach football match. The sand wasn't firm to stand on so you couldn't dribble. I was on the opposite side to Brian Carney and he kept taking the micky out of me. I'd had enough of this so I rattled into him. He got up with a mouth full of sand, "You little git".

Then there was go-kart racingand we also went out on four double masted yachts. Each team was on a yacht so we could have a race. The boats had engines to get us to the start line but when we got there it was like a lily pond. There was no wind whatsoever. I'm sure the people organising it knew beforehand that we weren't going to get a day of racing. They got on the tannoy informing us there was another option. There were quite a few crates of beer onboard so would that do? The lads were all delighted. The beers started going down then we saw some dolphins swimming nearby so of course, the lads started stripping off to dive in and join them. It finished up a good day with quite a few drunken bodies.

That night, we had a meal organised. A rugby union guy had come to our hotel saying he had a bar and would love the boys to come and have a drink so we agreed to visit the guys bar after our evening meal. It was a nice night so the players were able to drink outside on little tables. It was a good bar and the people there were really friendly. There was a gang of kids playing with a football so Brian Carney decided to join in. He was well away, so much so that Kris Radlinski took him back to the hotel. I think it was only about nine o clock.

During the series itself, England had a match at Wigan against Australia. Mobile phones were banned in the dressing room and I had left mine in my bag. I was going through my usual routine of getting everything ready before a big game when Mickey Higham told me, "Stan, your phone's going off".

"Damn," I replied going to my bag. I got it and went straight out of the dressing room. It was England team manager Phil Clarke. He told me he had a problem in that he was in a toilet at the ground but he had discovered there was no toilet roll. He said he was sat there with his pants round his ankles. He wanted me to go and get him some toilet roll. I went to a steward and got the toilet roll. I was shouting over the cubicles to finally hear, "I'm in here". He was grateful to say the least.

The outcome of that was that when anyone in the camp did anything untoward they had to do a forfeit back at the team hotel. The forfeit could be of their own choice. On the Tuesday night, these forfeits would have to be done in front of the rest of the group. As my phone had been seen in the dressing room, I had to do something. Phil felt responsible for ringing my phone so said he would join in with me.

My idea was something I had done for the family at Christmas in the past, dressing up as Freddie Mercury with lycra tights on. I had made three plywood guitars and painted them all. I also got hold of a set of drums. I spoke to Brian Noble who was the coach and explained about the forfeit but said I would need a backing group. Him and England doctor Brooksy agreed to be in the backing group. So, it was Brooksy on drums and me, Nobby and Clarkey on guitars. What I'd also done is made huge penises out of stockings so that we could stuff them down the lycra tights. We'd got a tape with a couple of Queen songs on. We had to perform that in front of all the lads and had them all joining in. This was filmed on the DVD believe it or not.

Watching that 2005 DVD brings back memories, even if Brian Carney's language on it is disgraceful. Maybe it's an Irish thing using the f word in every sentence. I think using it so often makes it lose its potency and impact. I hear players use it sparingly such as Jamie Peacock and it means that bit more. At half time in Saints' 11-10 play off defeat to Leeds in 2013, Jon Wilkin said, "We've got to come off that effing field with nothing left in us," and it hit home. Brian has to switch it off in his current role with Sky because it wouldn't look good if Eddie Hemmings asked what he thought of a try and replied with, "Effing tremendous". When I worked in the pit, you used the f word in every sentence. It was the language of the pit. I came home and never used that language in front of the kids. I switched it off.

The worst injury I have ever seen was Paul Deacon's horrific facial injury during that Tri Nations series. His palette had actually been dislodged. What the doctor Chris Brookes did after the game was incredible as it was a dangerous situation for Paul. The number of blood vessels that had been broken in the injury was a real concern.

I hit it off with Kevin Sinfield and Jamie Peacock straightaway. They are both fabulous players. I don't know what Jamie runs on. I wish I had half a glass of it. Also, if you ever go out for a meal with Sinny, you're in good company. He is a gentleman off the field. He plays the game straight and is a fantastic ambassador for the game. Both

Jamie and Sinny and also Rob Burrow come over and shake my hand after a Saints v Leeds game. There's only Ryan Bailey who has never spoken to me even though I was with him at international level. He didn't even say hello. I guess everyone is different.

I loved working with Barrie McDermott and Terry O'Connor. They were both jokers in the GB squad. I think that's how they've succeeded in the media. They are two great lads. Barrie was my type of player, he took knocks and he gave them. Everytime he met Stuart Fielden, sparks flew. It was old school.

I introduced Terry to Celia at Scully's wedding. His first words were, "Stan never gives me anything. He gives me less than he gives the other players and I don't think it's fair". After I finished refereeing, I noticed that Terry O'Connor could be the biggest con man on the pitch. If his side were winning, he would often waste time by feigning injury before a scrum. When meeting up with Barry and Terry, it's always a laugh and they are good company.

Terry Newton was another prankster. I would dish all the Great Britain kit out into bags for each player including sponsored leisurewear and training gear. The first time I put it out, Terry insisted I had only given him two pairs of shorts rather than the three he should have had. I gave him a spare pair until he tried to do it again. It then became a joke between us.

"Stan, you've only given me one vest".

"Terry, guess whose bag I packed first?" They try it on with you, I'm sure they've plenty of family and mates who'd love some Great Britain training kit. It's all part of the game.

I really hit it off with Andrew Farrell. I would often be the butt of a lot of jokes in international camp having been a referee and also being a kitman. I would often take my video camera with me to camp. I remember once in Marbella I was filming training when Andrew ran across shouting, "Stan, will you put some clothes on". He was a great guy and a good captain. I remember the big fight he had with Paul Sculthorpe during a Saints v Wigan derby at Knowsley Road. He always had that aggression in him even with a Great Britain team mate.

As a result of my work in the international setup and as recognition for my long years of service to the sport, I was invited to Buckingham Palace to a garden party. I was really looked forward to going to the Queen's garden party. I had my best bib and tucker ready. I was very excited to be going down. It was a beautiful day. We got to Buckingham Palace and had to queue up to have our passports checked by security. We went through into the grounds and there were thousands of people there. We didn't know what to expect so Celia and I were just milling about. There were large marquees everywhere. There were people in top hats and tails as you can imagine. There were people there from all different walks of life. There were two big bands with the Coldstream Guards playing in one marquee. The gardens are huge with lakes in them. We were looking for somewhere to sit and we found some little tables near a marquee.

There was an air force and a naval person sat there so we went over as I knew they would be like us, ordinary people. We got chatting to them about why each of us had been invited, and I explained mine was because of rugby league and that I had a grandson who played the game in the RAF. They asked me his name and they knew him which was such a coincidence. We did have a connection.

The Queen came out of the palace in the afternoon. It's all roped off where she walks through the gardens. The crowd stand right up to the ropes forming an avenue for the Queen to walk through. The nearest we got to her was about thirty metres away. It was a very tiring day but it was an absolute honour.

It was such a pleasure to be involved in the international set up. To be involved with Great Britain was great. One of my fondest memories is standing in a line with the players as part of the official squad photo. I remember when I was younger seeing those GB squad photos that were about three foot long up on a clubs wall with the players in a line and the manager in the middle. Never did I dream I would end up on one of those photos myself.

I had some great times with Great Britain and worked with some fantastic people such as David Waite and Brian Noble. I have really fond memories from those times. I know they say that you can't live on memories but they can't take them away from you either.

I finished with Great Britain of my own accord because of my family really. I've done some things I probably shouldn't have done like not going to my kids christenings. I was just rugby daft. The Saints season would finish in October then I would be with Great Britain. I was never going away on holiday as a result. I felt I was getting a bit old and knew I had to give something up. Celia told me to pack in at Saints but that wasn't happening. My last international match was when Great Britain played New Zealand at Knowsley Road which was fitting. In the dressing room afterwards, Brian Noble made a presentation to me of a signed shirt from all the lads. I wrote to the RFL explaining my decision and got a lovely letter back saying how they appreciated everything I had done.

It was time to move on and give a little bit back to my family.

20

On Reflection

The game is not dirty today as it used to be when I refereed but it is still physical. The players have to go ten metres back so the collision of players is harder plus the players are bigger, fitter and faster. They're in the gymnasium every day, they take the right supplements whereas in the part-time professional days, additional nutrition was a few pints.

I've seen both sides of rugby, the rough and often dirty era of years gone by where the likes of Jim Mills and Kevin Ashcroft thrived, through to the modern day where athletes like James Roby, Rob Burrow and Ryan Hall have the main influence in the game.

I do have to say though that I think today's game can be very predictable at times. It can be five drives and a kick with seemingly most tries coming from kicks these days. Handling skills today are sensational though with the Jamie Lyon type pass being practiced by a number of different players. I'm glad I've been involved with both types of game.

The game has changed greatly. When I first came to Saints, players like Alan Hunte would have a cigarette after the game, you don't see that today. Silk Cut were cup sponsors and would come to the dressing room with 500 cigs!

When I was at the colliery, loads of the miners smoked. They obviously couldn't smoke down the mine so would chew tobacco instead. I tried it but could never get into it. As soon as they came up the mine, before they even had a wash, many were straight to their locker to get their cigs out and have a smoke.

When I got into amateur refereeing, it was with local clubs like Leigh Miners, Thatto Heath and Pilkington Recs. The amateurs would try to emulate what was going on in the professional game. They were hard, physical games. I wouldn't have neutral touch judges then at that level. It would be one from the home side and one from the away so I got no help at all. That was a good apprenticeship for me and helped me hone my skills. I don't think today's referees go through the same thing. However they are getting in referees from the age of 12 which is a good thing.

Looking back, we had some strong characters as referees. There was Dennis Davies who always had a short back and sides and refused to referee games on a Sunday when.

There was Joe Manley who we called "Play On" Joe. A fight would start and he would let it go on. He'd eventually stop play and ask who had started the fight. He'd then award the penalty.

We had a large group of about 20-odd referees back then available for games every weekend. There was Lindop, Campbell, Holdsworth, Thompson, myself and many more. Today we only have about seven to pick from each week for Super League.

Nowadays the way referees sometimes dress is appalling. We have them in pink and blue or with draught boards on the front and back. They look a right state. I look at officials in other sports such as football and rugby union. If we put all the officials in a line and said, "Pick the stupid one," it would be rugby league every time. We were like policemen back in the day, always wearing black.

I could see the logic in referees going full-time to get everything knocked into shape. However, with televised games, they get so much support from the screen that a lot of the work is done for them. I don't think them going full-time has improved the standard of refereeing. We've lost one or two through it going full-time such as Karl Kirkpatrick, who was a decent referee but had a good job outside the game.

With the lack of mixing with players and coaches after the game and the ability to discuss decisions gone, they have isolated themselves and made themselves an elite group. I don't like saying, "When we were lads, it was better," but I think in this case it's appropriate. Referees today seem to lack personality and there is little in the way of player relationship. When I see a game where a referee goes to the video screen on eight occasions for tries, it's something I cannot believe. The referees don't speak to anybody after the game; they'll sit together on a table after the match and not mix. I also don't like the recent innovation of the referee wearing a camera on his head making him look like a demented dalek.

I think Ben Thaler's ok. He has something about him. I watch a lot of the NRL and I think their system of operating with two referees in a match is working very well. One is on every tackle and the other is back with the defensive line.

Supporters would be amazed at what the players have to put up with at certain grounds in the game today. It's been said for a while that Castleford and Wakefield need to develop. I'll use Cas as an example. Inside the dressing room are two little urinals. There are three toilets along the corridor. That's for two teams of 17 plus officials. There are players queuing up. Then once we've set all the kit up, we can't get back in the room because it's not big enough to hold the team and the staff. Those clubs badly need to develop their facilities. Don't get me wrong, they are good clubs that I love.

As for my role today, on a match day, it's my job to get the kit ready before the game. I used to have to clean all the boots every Monday morning. Since we moved to Langtree Park we have changed to a system where the lads now bring all their own boots. We insist that they have at least two pairs, one with moulded studs and one with screw in studs. I'm always available to change studs for players. We set out fruit, bottled water, energy drinks, Jaffa Cakes and wine gums. I think the coaching and backroom staff eat more wine gums than the players. We have masseurs on hand and every player is rubbed before every game. Then there's strapping players up. I think the strapping bill is the biggest one at the club. They do a cracking job though when you see them get on the pitch and attend to a player with a cut. We get all the balls ready to the right pressure. In hot weather, we have an ice box filled with small towels.

Langtree Park is a fantastic stadium. The dressing rooms are identical which is required for hosting international fixtures. We have an additional room connected to the home dressing room for the players to warm up in with artificial turf in it. It's a great setup. The only thing from a kitman's point of view is that the washing room for the kit is behind the posts, up at the top in the West Stand which means a hell of a trek with the kit. Fortunately that's Alan Clarke's job now. The corporate facilities are second to none though. It's all through the chairman Eamonn McManus with the help of the rest of the Board. He's worked hard for the club. The amount of time and money he has put into the club is phenomenal.

I only do two days a week now. My partnership with Alan Clarke works well and we know exactly what we are doing when it comes to captains run and game day. We both know our own jobs including me making sure there is a clock up in the dressing room.

Current coach Nathan Brown is better than Simmons was in the respect of keeping us involved a bit and he will have a chat to staff.

I do feel that the Joynt, Cunningham, Sculthorpe era were the last days of when I felt truly involved with things. I don't really have many close relationships with the players at Saints now. The ice has never fully broken with some of them and I'm not down the training pitch every day like I used to be. There are some I have a laugh and a chat with.

The James Roby's of this world, I don't know that they are there in the dressing room. He never asks me for a thing. James Roby is a gentleman in the dressing room, and if he wants anything he'll say please which you don't get from everyone. After a game, most players will just chuck their kit onto the floor which is fair enough. James doesn't do that. He will put his kit the right way and put it on the table for me. It's obviously the way he has been brought up.

I really like Tommy Makinson, he's a really friendly kid even though I am appalled by his lime green boots. He came in the dressing room one day to grab some food off the table. I knew it was his debut so I said, "Tommy, it's your first match which means you are allowed one wine gum. Next week, you can have two wine gums. If you can put a run of five games together, we'll review it". We had a good laugh and we've built up a great rapport since then. I did the same thing with young Swifty.

Looking back on my life in rugby, I know there have been some tremendous players with great careers who never played at Wembley such as John Woods. I'm lucky enough to have been seven times in two different roles. I went to Wembley twice as a reserve official and have been back five times with Saints with the club winning all five.

I've also been to Old Trafford nine times for the Grand Final with Saints. We won four and then lost five in a row.

There's also been the two World Club Championship wins over Brisbane. How many players have been to that many finals?

Writing this book has been hard work but when I was putting it together I realised just how many good people I've met over the years. Another good thing about doing this book is that it made me start thinking more about some of the stuff we did as kids.

My wife Celia has had to live with my passion for rugby league all her life. She reckons we've been married 50-odd years and she's seen me 10, which makes a happy marriage.

Rugby league was always my life. I never saw any of my grandchildren christened because I was refereeing at the time. Kick off's then were Sunday 3pm so I said "They can get christened without me". I've got called for that ever since. Even now they're grown up my grandkids still give me stick over it.

My rugby was in my spare time but it was my passion. I ate, slept and drank rugby, I still do. People ask me, "When are you packing in Wally?"

"When my legs'll not go," is my reply.

I work on an unpaid basis for Saints these days and just do the job for pleasure.

I have two children: Dean and Sharon. They both have a boy and a girl of their own. Sharon has Garry and Nicola. Dean had Craig and Lauren. I have four great grandchildren, all boys. There's Aaron, Oliver, Tom and Coby. The only one of the group who followed me into rugby was Garry. Craig was a fantastic golfer but put it to one side when he went to university. Garry started with Leigh Rangers. He was very bright but when he left school, he didn't want to go to university. I asked him if he thought about the forces. We had a guy at Saints called Gordon Pennington who was ex RAF. I got him to have a chat with our Garry who finished up in the RAF. He's never looked back since and has loved every minute of it. He carried on with his rugby whilst in the RAF. He's served in Iraq and Qatar.

The rest of them all love watching rugby too. Dean and Craig are at every Saints home match. Sharon and her husband Kevin are Wigan supporters which means Garry is. The rivalry of it all is interesting. When we went to one of the Grand Final's against Leeds, the two of them wanted the Rhinos to win. I told them they would never get another drink in my house again.

My grandson Garry played for the combined services in 2010 on their tour of Australia. They beat them in test matches over there. I was really proud of him because no matter what level it's at, beating the Aussies is always a real achievement. He was serving in Afghanistan in 2013 and they brought him back two weeks early to start training for test matches over here.

When I reflect on my upbringing and my time down the pit, I don't think young people today appreciate what they have. I don't think they realise what older generations didn't have that they take for granted. I never had a holiday until I was 16 and that was only Butlins which at the time I thought was the best holiday ever. I was able to take my kids away to Spain at a very early age. Then after that, they've been to Disney World. I tell the grandkids that to improve on what they have had in their life they'll have to take their children to the moon on holiday. When we talk about Christmas presents, the kids make fun of me. They don't know which box to open first as they get that much stuff. Christmas for me was my Dad making me a train. He'd get one of the wooden pit props, he'd cut a piece off, use a bobbin as a chimney and then use four more bobbins as wheels. The kids repeat that to me every year prefacing it with "When you were a lad, all you got was ..."

Parents these days are taxi drivers to their kids, taking them to training, taking them to school. Our Craig once rang me one night as his mum and dad weren't there. He wanted to know if I could give him a lift to the Hare and Hounds. That pub is literally half a mile away from where he lives. He said he should have been there to meet his mates five minutes ago. Alex Murphy wouldn't have beat me for anger down the phone at him. I lost it completely, I went for him. I told him never to ring me for anything like that again, I told him never to be late for anything either. He's turned out to be a belting lad. He's got a masters degree and now works at Media City and also appears on 5 Live.

As I've neared the end of this book I've given a few thoughts as to how I would like to be remembered. I hope it's as an integral part of any of the teams I've been involved in and that I've added something to them. And I genuinely hope I've been able to add a little bit of fun alongside attention to detail and making the team run more efficiently, whether that's in Mines Rescue, refereeing, or with Great Britain RL or in my time at Saints

I'm 79 now and with being retired I need to have an interest and doing the two days a week at Saints is that interest. It's too late in life for me to take up golf. I'll keep going at Saints until my health fails or they no longer want me. I do it for nothing and I keep going. I'm no longer making it my very first priority as I have done for the majority of my life. With Celia's 80th birthday in 2013, I had the family calling me as I couldn't do certain dates for the party because of Saints commitments. She'll be 81 by the time we have the party. Celia's happy for me to keep going at Saints because as she says, "I'm glad to get you out of the house for a bit".

The Saints spectators have been fantastic in my time with the club – especially the ones who stand behind the posts at away games. On a number of occasions when they've spotted me at a game they have sung out "There's Only One Stan Wall". It's times like that that make me feel very humble. When I refereed I always got the boos but it's a tremendous feeling to know how much the speckies think of me, I can't thank them enough.

I've made some terrific friends in rugby league and I continue to do so. I'm also still meeting up with people from the era I refereed.

I went from working down the pit for £2.50 an hour in hellish conditions, yet still enjoying the camaraderie of men I found in the bowels of the earth to being on top of the world working in the game I love. I wouldn't swap my journey for anything and the advice I would give anyone wanting to follow their dreams is to just do it. Put plenty of hard work in so that any hard times that you face will be overcome and enjoy the friendships you make along the way.

Tributes

Shaun Mcrae

The first time I met Stan was when I did some guest coaching at St Helens in 1995. I wasn't able to work with the Australian team in the 1995 World Cup because the Super League-ARL war. I had been with the Kangaroos between 1992 and 1994. In 1995, I accepted a role as assistant coach with New Zealand under Frank Endacott. After the World Cup, I was asked to stay on as a consultant or guest coach at St Helens. I was asked to have a look at their structures to see if I could have any input. I was at the club for a two week period then.

Stan always came across as an extremely professional man. He was always willing to share stories and had plenty to talk about. He was very thorough in his job. He was always willing to help and always seemed to be on the end of a brush. He was very fastidious and conscientious. He was very proud to be involved at St Helens. He took a lot of pride and passion in what he did.

When I first met Stan, I wasn't really aware of his past. I didn't know he had been a referee although it didn't take him long to let me know he had been. It might have been his second sentence to me. You found out a lot about Stan pretty quickly.

When I went back to Saints taking the head coach role in 1996, Stan was still there and is still at the club today. He's a bit of an icon, not only at the club but also in the game.

At Saints, Stan had to be a bit of a jack of all trades. That still applies in many respects at some clubs. We've moved on so much in some areas yet other areas have stagnated. The kitman role is so much more than that, it's a far more varied role. It wasn't just a case of ordering the kit for players. They are as much a piece of the pie as anyone else is. They are a very important cog in the wheel. Without people like Stan Wall, it puts a lot of pressure on other people.

It's a difficult role to try and do a job description for. There are kind of no boundaries to the role. "That'll be a job for Stan," would be a phrase often heard.

Stan would never tell you something wasn't his job; he would just get on with it. He had respect and he loved the club. He didn't want to let anyone down. There was nothing you could throw at Stan that would ever worry him. He commanded respect from everyone, players included.

Stan thrived on it all. He really enjoyed being part of it. He would be there every day at the club. I believe every club needs a Stan Wall.

Life always brings a combination of success and failure. When you have success, everybody wants to pat you on your back, everybody wants to shake your hand, everybody wants to tell you what a great job you're doing. I think it's the tough times, when you find out who your real friends and real supporters are. Stan was absolutely brilliant to me whether we won or lost. He probably taught me a little bit about emotion. I always came across as a fairly unemotional type of person. People used to say to me that they'd see me on the screen during a game and I wouldn't seem too excited. I would never seem to get too concerned or upset about things. I think I did very well to hide my emotions. Stan was quite similar during matches. He would go about his business at half time. If we had lost, after the match he was very much of the attitude of tomorrow's another day, we'll get on with it, we've got another game coming up.

There could be times where we'd lose a couple on the trot and the team wouldn't be playing so well. There were people at the club who would understand it and Stan was one of them. He'd been around the game for a long, long time. He was very loyal and supportive. They're the sort of people that you need, not just at the best of times but also when you are under pressure. Stan was terrific in that period for me.

One funny thing I recall is in relation to Stan's hearing issues. A lot of people used to accuse him of being deaf when he refereed, as well as having sight problems. It was when David Howes was chief executive and we had a sponsorship arrangement with Mizuno. The head of Mizuno's marketing had come for a meeting at the club and Stan was there with his little pad and pen. He was ready to make notes for all the orders for the squad. The deal didn't just cover kit but trainers and casual wear.

The meeting must have gone on for about an hour. David Howes had been listing how much we needed of each particular item. Stan was looking very attentive. After an hour, David closed the meeting and asked if everybody was happy. Stan replied, "When are we going to get to the orders?"

"We've done it all," replied David. "Haven't you been writing it down?"

"No," said Stan, "I've been waiting". He still had a blank pad.

To this day, me and Stan still shake hands and talk. For me, that's the sign of what I like about people. When I worked with Stan, I used to refer to him as the kitman. I never did when I left though because for me, he had become a friend. That's the most important thing to me in this business. I'm delighted to be able to call Stan a friend of mine. I'm delighted that he's been able to put his story down and share it with other people. He's had a very colourful and often unusual career. There have been some high profile players and high profile coaches yet Stan has achieved so much quietly. People have the right to be able to hear about it. Hopefully, I've been able to play a small role in being able to portray what sort of man Stan Wall is.

Everything I've said about Stan comes from the heart. He's a wonderful man, a family man with great ethics. He has a high moral fibre and is a great worker. The testament for me is that he is still at St Helens now. The proof in any walk of life is longevity. That sums up people for me.

Brian Bowman

Stan was one of many characters in the game back then when I was Leigh chairman. We all had a lot of fun although Stan was probably grateful he didn't get to referee Leigh the way I interacted with certain officials.

Kenny Spencer was refereeing his first televised game and it was at Leeds. This stray dog got on the pitch. It followed Kenny around for a good twenty minutes. They'd have a scrum and the dog would go and sit at the side of it. Shortly after that, Kenny refereed a game at Leigh. For a joke, I put a bowl of dog biscuits, a bowl of water and a lead in the referee's room.

Bill Fiddes was a touch judge and after one game he came in for refreshments, I told the tea lady that she would have to put the cup in his hand. "Why?" she asked.

"Because he's a blind bastard" I said. He reported me to the RFL for that remark.

Stan was a good referee in an era when the game could be very tough. If I had to list the worst referees, this book would be longer than *War and Peace*.

Brian Noble

Stan sent me off at Odsal in my playing days and cost me two test matches. I deserved to get sent off by the way. I think I'd been fighting with Kevin Tamati, and that was my first experience of Stan. He sent me off in a very pleasant manner, "Get off".

When I was Great Britain coach, Stan fulfilled the role of kitman and all round good egg. You need those kind of people in your camp. Players gravitate to people like him. We had a sports psychologist but I said we didn't need one because if a player had a problem he'd tell Stan and Stan would tell everyone else. All of a sudden, it wasn't a problem. That was what Stan provided for us, he was a good barometer. If you asked Stan an honest question, you would always get an honest answer. We had a similar view on rugby league.

Stan had a list for everything. He was meticulous in his preparation. We were trying to create something initially with David Waite and then with me, something very special and we managed to do that. Stan helped make the shirt a very proud thing to possess again. To do that, you didn't just hand out a shirt, you had to be part of a group of people who believed in international rugby and the fact that they were working with the best people which we were.

Stan's energy and enthusiasm is a reminder of why you should do something. He absolutely passionately believes in what he does. That's why he's still around at St Helens. If you love something truly and deeply, you'll do it. That's another reminder for the modern player. You bounce off energetic, enthusiastic people like Stan because of their commitment to the job.

He's good at finding out when issues are weighing heavily on people. As good as we all like to think we are, sometimes you need a helping hand. I've been all over the world with Stan and sometimes it would just be one sentence from him that would galvanise me. In tricky situations he's there as well as in the good times. He's not a fair weather friend; he's an all weather friend. He has helped me out immeasurably over the years.

Sometimes people lose touch with reality and by that I mean, we sometimes forget how lucky we are in doing what we do. There are a lot of people in very different circumstances to ourselves, whether that be a disability or a tough working life. Stan would often hold court at the end of the day and tell tales of derring do and bravado. He reminded the players of the reality of a working life. It was good to remind them of where the game has come from and the type of people who have been involved in the game over the years.

Brian Carney

St Helens have been lucky to have Stan involved with their club. I was certainly lucky when I was playing with Great Britain and Ireland to have him as a kitman there.

He was a good man to have around the GB camp. He was always bright and bubbly. Anytime anyone was moaning, Stan would nip it in the bud. He'd then moan even longer and tell them they didn't know they were born by telling them about his experiences in the coal mines, telling them that his mum would feed the whole family with one piece of bacon – the bacon would touch the bread and that would be their bacon sandwiches. The father would have the bacon, Stan and the rest would have a whiff of it on their bread.

He's a great character, one of the biggest compliments I could pay him is that when you're in camp you look for the friendly faces and Stan was always one of the first ones you'd look for. He was never down.

We were doing a pre tournament training camp in Porta Banus. We were staying in a nice place in the hills outside Marbella. We had great training facilities there and a good hotel. We had a free day and on that night there were some challenges set such as getting your photograph taken with a policeman. We were split into groups for these challenges. It was a really good way of getting everybody together. We were all mixed up out of our club groups. Stan and the coaches were each put in a different group too. One of the challenges was bringing an old lady back with us. We decided we would get Stan dressed up as a lady, took him to a very nice boutique and got him kitted out. I have to say, from behind, Stan Wall in a dress is not a bad sight. I think we got top points for that one.

He's a champion and rugby league is lucky to have a personality like him involved in the game, he's a great bloke.

Ian Millward

Stan is a smiling bloke who was always good for the organisation. I think everybody appreciated his input and his presence.

My first time with Stan was in a room when I walked in to meet everybody at the club for the first time. There were a host of good players in there. Stan came up to my office at the end of the day with two big bags of training gear. He was very welcoming and was a good face to have around. We wanted the staff to have passion for rugby league and passion for the job. They had to have an attitude of being able to work hard outside the call of duty. Stan was all that. He was very pleasant and keen for both the club and myself to do well.

Because he had been around a while and probably because he had been a referee too he had a side of him that was disciplined. He didn't take any rubbish off any of the younger guys. A lot of the senior guys and leaders in the group like Chris Joynt liked that. Stan was always helpful but also respected in his role. That first season, I didn't have an assistant coach until the play offs as I wanted to be really hands on myself, Stan was full-time and we had a full-time strength and conditioning coach and a full-time analysis person. That was it in terms of full-time staff.

It's paramount to have the right people behind the scenes to achieve the sort of success that we did at the time. They've got to be able to handle the good days. They can't be too giddy or excited on the big days. We used to talk about the body language of the staff and how it was so important. How they held themselves and how they portrayed themselves around the players was vital. If they had the attitude of "this is going to be a hard game, we're going to struggle" it can negatively effect the players. We always used to try and portray a sense of confidence amongst the staff. Stan's office was right next to the players' dressing room. He had so much contact with them before and after training.

I used like getting into the club early, about half past seven in a morning. Stan would be having a brew and I'd sit down there and have a chat with him.

Stan's got heaps of tales, when we went on pre-season training camps or we stayed overnight somewhere before a big game, I always liked the staff to get together that night and have a couple of quiet drinks and reflect on the week. We'd savour the moment before a big occasion. We never went over the top as we wouldn't want to be like that in front of the players. Stan would always be part of the conversation when we got together like that.

David Waite

When I took over as Great Britain head coach, I had to put a group of people together. We were looking for people with unique qualities and experience. When you take over, you want to try and get a club feel as well as something new for the players. All of a sudden, they had someone from overseas who had been flown in and given the job of trying to get the Ashes back. We wanted the highest quality people possible on our backroom staff. My research and questions led me to Stan. I had identified some key leaders within the group and some of those people were at St Helens. When you're new to the job, you use every resource available to you to identify people who had the potential to fulfill certain roles. We found Stan as the most outstanding character and the most able person to carry out the role Stan needed to carry out within the group. Everything in his job description would be calm, therefore the players would be calm. Little did I know at that stage the unique qualities that he had.

He obviously had something because everybody you

spoke to spoke about him in glowing terms and how valuable he was. His longevity was a pretty key issue for me because longevity meant stability.

I think it's lovely that this book has been put together for such a special fella. He's an absolute treasure.

He's such a great role model. It's his life experiences and where he has come from that I thought were just fantastic for young men representing their country to listen to.

He would tell his mining tales and it wouldn't just be those of us with a little bit of grey on our head that were fascinated. He did hold court a number of times. He had a great ability to mix within a group with people of all ages at any stage of the day. He's pretty unflappable.

The stories of him at the coalface and the history of the people who were doing what he did, to have a look at him he's as fit as, in our terms, a mallee bull. He was incredible and he became a vital ingredient in what we set about doing. He did things with as much enthusiasm as a young person would do it with.

He's a cracking fella and I've certainly got some fond memories of spending time with him. The quality of the person is remarkable. That happened at breakfast, lunch and dinner. That happened over a beer when we won, it happened over a beer when we lost. There was always a calming, soothing experienced person around. He's seen lots of things in the sport, therefore things tended to sail on an even keel. When things did get rocky, he wasn't a bad sounding board either. He'd always give you a nod or a wink or an "hmm" to let you know what he was thinking. He's a special person. There's not many of them around.

Chris Joynt

Stan has been synonymous with Saints' most successful era. Eric Hughes brought him in 1995 as he certainly had the experience of being involved in a team environment at Leigh and his refereeing days.

He is a great character. From my point of view and that of my team mates at the time who were seasoned internationals, he treated everybody as equals. I hold him in such high respect for that.

He was also good at tale telling from the life experiences he's had from his days down the pit which he never shuts up about. I found it kind of interesting because some of the players I played with, and certainly players today, can't even dream about what went on down there. They were tough days and some tough men.

I would socialise with Stan and put the world to rights with him when away in camp. No matter his age, still to this day, he's as fit as a butcher's dog. We thought he was older than a conker tree when he started at the club, I've been retired ten years now and he's still going.

Stan had a lisp at one point due to new teeth which he had for about three weeks. Everytime he spoke, we couldn't stop laughing. It was like a lisp cum whistle.

Stan loved to go on holidays with Celia but when he retired from mining, he went onto travel the world with what he loves best: the sport of rugby league. He enjoys what he does. He always put himself after the team.

The dedication he showed at Saints was the reason he got brought into the international setup. That was more travelling for him.

Everybody at the club complemented each other. I was captain of the team as Stan was captain of his backroom team. All the guys from Gibbsy, Alan Clarke, the masseurs Ian and Derek, all those people were invaluable to us.

He had to look after boots and kit for over twenty people. It's certainly a pressure job because in the heat of the battle, Stan needed to provide whatever a player wanted.

Eric Hughes

Stan refereed me many times when I played for Widnes. As you know, I always got on well with referees. His personality came through in his refereeing. He knew what he was doing and his communication levels were good with the players. He was a referee you were able to chat to. I thought the best referees were those who allowed a dialogue between themselves and players. Stan came into that category.

Stan was good for Leigh because he had various roles within the club. Everyone knew him as a kitman but he also qualified as a rugby league coach. He was useful in many, many ways. As a coach, I always wanted people around me who had a great work ethic. Stan is a hard worker and his integrity is second to none. He is from the heartlands of rugby league. He is quite willing to work many, many hours. If you worked out the hourly rate for people like Stan with the hours they put in, they'd be on a pittance. It was all for the love of the game and the love of the club. He'd often help me set up training. He'd bring some ideas to training.

I found Stan so useful to Leigh that I consequently brought him to St Helens with me. He was so much more than a kitman. I could always discuss things with him. Within the fabric of the club you've got people like him who are working hard who love the game and love the club. The more people like that you get within a club, the better the club's going to be.

If you could bottle Stan's energy, you would make a fortune. I know he cuts the lawns for people in his neighbourhood who are younger than him yet he refers to them as "old folk". His attitude is that if he stays in his chair, he'll be frightened to get out of it. He walks, he cycles, he works.

Barrie McDermott

In the 2001 Ashes series, I got to know Stan really well as he was our kitman. Having been in the game a long time, I know you've got to make friends straightaway with two people; the kitman and the physio. You need both of them to be on your side. If you've got a bump or bruise, you need the physio to help you deal with it or maybe help you shield the injury from the coach. That was always my intention so I didn't miss out. With the kitman, being a bigger bloke, I needed to make sure my kit fitted me. I was always particular about my numbers as well. I wanted number 10 but I didn't like 8 as I had a superstition about it. With my kit, I wanted it to be loose without it being gigantic. I wasn't the tallest at five foot ten and I didn't want a dress but I didn't want a crop top either. Stan was a good ally. Getting to know him, I realised he was a good soul.

It was during the 2003 series with Australia though that I had my most memorable incident with Stan. I had the two funniest blokes throughout my career with me then: Adrian Morley and Tez Newton. We'd all played together in our early days at Leeds. We all tormented the life out of each other. We all wound each other up and would be playing tricks on each other. Throw Terry O'Connor into that and it was a real funny mix. If you bore the brunt of it, you were really suffering.

We'd lost the first test by four points, we then lost the second test over at Hull. The third test was a dead rubber. Everybody was in a really bad mood. We were all stressed as it looked like we were going to get whitewashed. We were desperately brokenhearted and Stan was more in charge of morale than logistics at this point. He was always trying to get people to smile. In the last training run, Tez Newton had told Stan, "Baz looks like he's flagging a bit there Stan, can you get him some Jaffa Cakes?"

Stan, being in charge of morale, looked at Tez Newton, went out of the ground and bought me some Jaffa Cakes. He returned and was stood on the side of the pitch with an open packet of Jaffa Cakes. What Stan didn't know was that Tez Newton, Adrian Morley and Terry O'Connor had been absolutely savaging me for 48 hours about my weight. They said my kit was too tight, I looked a bit pale in the face, and did I need something to eat.

We were playing an Academy side in this opposed training session. After a particularly poor period in this session where I knocked on, we headed over to the sidelines for a drink of water after harsh words from the coaching staff. In the middle of Andrew Farrell giving us a speech about us sorting it out, Stan, at the top of his voice, shouts, "Barry, do you want a Jaffa Cake?"

I turned round, I looked at Stan and said, "Are you taking the piss or what?"

"No, no, the lads think you look like you're flagging a bit. Do you need some energy?"

"Stan, get stuffed".

Stan scuppered off, tail between his legs. Tez Newton and Terry O'Connor were crying with laughter. I realised by looking at them two and the other numpty Morley just exactly what had gone on.

I spent the next 48 hours apologising to Stan, asking him if he wanted a brew and asking him if he was ok. Everytime I see Stan, I still think of him stood there with hound dog eyes, Jaffa Cakes in his hand and me telling him to where to go.

Stan Wall is an example to everybody that plays the game that you can still be relevant and still contribute in so many different ways. Unfortunately, ex players and ex coaches get lost to the game because they can't find somewhere to get involved. What we love when we play is being involved in and part of a team and the banter that goes with it. When you're not the main man, kicking goals, scoring tries, making tackles, it's hard to find your place in that. Stan did it as a referee and people talk about how he used humour in that role to make tough calls and to make very violent, vicious people listen to him. He's still managed to keep his humour in the varying roles he's had since his refereeing heyday. He's still managed to have that Ray French sweep hairstyle. He's still been the butt of everybody's joke but come back with a really fast quip and a really fast riposte. That's why everybody loves him.

The day Stan Wall isn't around the Saints club and he isn't the first person you see when you get there to greet everybody with that thick Leyther accent will be a sad day indeed.

Alex Murphy

Stan worked down the pit and that was bad enough. It was very tough, and he used to come to training with his mining gear still on sometimes. You couldn't imagine him doing that job not being the biggest of people but he worked on the coalface. Put it this way, when I went down the pit, by the time they told me where I was going I had packed in.

When I took the coaching job at Leigh, Stan asked me if he could take part in our training sessions, I said as long as he didn't get involved in things that were very important to the side that it wouldn't be a problem. He was quite keen. At the end of each training session we would always have a game of touch and pass and he loved that. We put him on the wing and that's how he learned how to run. It kept him in touch with the lads who were the sort of people he would be refereeing as he began his career. It also kept his fitness levels very high. He was a good trainer actually. He thoroughly enjoyed it and people got to know him.

One of David Chisnall's strong points was that he wanted to catch wingmen. Stan went flying down the wing and Chis was obviously thinking he could get him. However, he didn't want to tick him, he wanted to kill him. Stan soon learned that could sometimes happen in rugby league. You never take for granted how quick a lad is.

He has worked hard in everything he has done and taken a pride in it. He was a first class referee, a nice bloke to talk to, he was very honest and if you had a problem with something he did and told him he wouldn't hold grudges. Not all the referees were like that. Stan would advise me of certain ways to handle certain referees and what their strengths and weaknesses were.

He's a born and bred Leyther. There was a fella there called Jackie Burn and he was my assistant. Stan and Jackie were always talking; Jackie was a lovely man who had come through the A team. Stan was always happy to pitch in.

One thing that does stand out was that the lads were always hiding Stan's gear. One of his boots would have been hid in the A team dressing room, one in the referee's room. Stan took everything in his stride including the time the players threw him in the bath.

Joe Walsh was always taking the mickey out of him and would sometimes go out on the field with Stan's refereeing gear on. It was also good when we had a player sent off, the report would come into the club and we would always run it by Stan for his advice. He was always helpful.

There was a hill just outside of Warrington where we would sometimes train. It was about two miles and the incline was tremendous. They would have to run up and down it in a certain time. Stan thrived in that situation and would come into his own. He had lads twice as fit as him but he loved the competition. He did exceptionally well.

Nobody can tell me they know everything about rugby league, sometimes other people know something that you don't. I'm not too proud to ask anybody for knowledge, if somebody could help me I would ask them. That's why Stan became my assistant coach at Leigh for a spell. Stan was a nice bloke, very amenable and easy to get on with. You could talk to him and I did.

Stan has had a tremendous time in the game; he's worked hard for a lot of people and done exceptionally well. I have nothing but respect for the guy.

Paul Wellens

Kitman doesn't do Stan's role justice, he's had his hand in just about everything. He's probably filled every role at the club during his time at Saints.

The more I've got to know Stan at the club the more questions I've asked him. He tells his tales of life down the pit. It's always interesting to hear his tales. Lads always bounce ideas off him. He's always really funny as well, putting us young lads in our place.

It's essential to have people like Stan behind the scenes; you can't do without those people. As players, what we need to be able to do is get into the gym, onto the training pitch or onto the pitch itself and just do our job. We can only do that if everything else has been taken care of by the backroom staff. We've been lucky that over the years at St Helens we've had a number of hardworking people in those roles who have just got on with the job and provided for the players. Stan is certainly one of them.

One of the real plus points of Stan and something that everybody enjoys is the fact that he always has a smile on his face. As a player, you don't bounce into training every day with a smile on your face. Some days, you're tired or you might be coming off the back of a loss. One thing that was consistent with Stan was when you came in, he'd always make you feel better about yourself. He'd crack a joke.

There was a group of young lads talking about girls in the dressing room, and one of them asked Stan, "When you was young, did you lot used to chase women?"

"The trouble with you young lads, tha thinks you invented shagging."

It was a genius line and it had everybody cracking up.

Mick Morgan

Back in my playing days, the referees didn't want to be the star attraction. They would just referee the game and you could talk to them. You could also have a beer with them after the game.

Stan was a top bloke. His main aim was to keep twenty six players on the field if he could. When the game was finished, he'd want spectators to be talking about the players not the referee. They weren't well paid back then. Referees would turn up and do the job and we wouldn't have had a game without them. They were approachable too. You'd get to know how they refereed the game and they got to know things about us as players too. You always knew it would be called straight down the middle if Stan was in charge of the game.

Ronnie Campbell

I first met Stan through refereeing, we became friends. He got promoted the year before me and was my big pal in the refereeing world.

If I didn't have a match, very often I would go with Stan to watch his game. Stan was involved in the very first trial by TV in the sport. He refereed Hull KR v Widnes at Hull KR. I had gone with him to the game. Roy Holdstock of Hull KR elbowed Andy Gregory off the ball. He dropped him like a stone. Les Gorley of Widnes ran in and cracked Holdstock. Stan hadn't seen it but it had been caught on television. After the game in the car, Stan asked me what had kicked it off. I told him about it saying that there was no way he could have seen it on the pitch. Holdstock ended up being hauled up in front of the disciplinary committee. That was the very first trial by TV.

Stan was a very good referee. He never refereed at Wembley which was a shame. The two of us would swap places, I'd do a big game then he'd do a big game. He was reserve referee at Wembley. The RFL had brought in a silly rule that if the referee hadn't experienced Wembley they couldn't referee there. So if you were made reserve referee for the cup final one year, you were more or less automatically guaranteed to be the referee the year after. I told the hierarchy I thought it was stupid because a referee who has had an excellent season knows he can't referee at Wembley for at least another twelve months. Another reason it was daft was that the players in a cup final didn't have to get to experience Wembley before playing there. They dropped it after a few seasons. Stan was reserve referee at Wembley for the Hull v Hull KR final yet didn't get the final the year after.

When I got the 84-85 final, I was working in St Helens with Dave Chisnall at the time. The first person to ring me was Eric Clay who always called me young man, he said, "Congratulations young man, I told you 10 years ago you'd referee at Wembley one day".

The next phone call was from Stan, in his final season as I was in my penultimate one, to congratulate me.

I really felt for him. It was brilliant to have my best mate in refereeing as my reserve for the final. We were there on their big day together. You would have thought there would have been a bit of resentment or jealousy on his part but he was absolutely brilliant. He helped me all weekend. We had a smashing time down there. At Wembley, Stan was behind me in the tunnel and I was getting a bit excited, he was telling me to calm down. I nearly went out too early as everything was timed but Stan pulled me back.

But Stan did get the last match of the season, the Premiership Final between St Helens and Hull KR at Elland Road, I went there to see his last match as a referee. We had a good night in the Greyhound after that and that was Stan finished.

Paul Sculthorpe

Stan is a great character who I first encountered when I signed for Saints in 1998. He'd do anything for the players. He was a real good presence to be about. He had quite a calming influence on people. I always had a great relationship with him and had a good craic with him. We would take the mickey out of each other.

I would only ever play in clean boots and would never leave my boots with the kitmen so they could stick them in the dry room for them to come back like concrete. Stan would always wind me up about that.

People like Stan were a massive part of the club's success, all the preparation that goes into what you see on the field. If you go into a game and don't feel like everything has been prepared correctly, it can have a massive negative impact on you. We were very fortunate to have people like Stan and Alan Clarke, you could see they thoroughly enjoyed what they did. They did their job immaculately every time. They were good people as well.

When I was goal kicker at Saints, Stan would bring the kicking tee on for me. He'd always have something to say to me, a real calming influence. Hopefully he has now forgiven me for what I repeatedly used to do to him in the dressing room. Stan used to spend ages combing his hair, it looked like a ducks arse at the back. I'd wait until he had spent fifteen minutes in the mirror then I'd put my fingers right through his hair messing it up. He used to look like one of them kid's troll figures. I used to call him "The Troll". Eventually he came in with a skinhead and looked at me saying, "That's for you so you can't mess my hair anymore".

Stan would always have a tale to tell. He's done a lot in his life and he looks fantastic for his age. You can see he's always been a get up and at 'em person.

Phil Clarke

Stan was part of the GB setup for several years. In professional sports, I think you have a lot of people who don't have a lot of depth of character. All some of them have ever done is play their chosen sport, not many have had jobs. Stan's value was the grey hairs that he had. He'd been a coal miner, he'd seen a bit of life, he'd been around, he's got grandkids. That wisdom and experience was really useful in keeping people's feet on the ground and putting things into perspective.

He also brought a tremendous amount of enthusiasm and positivity. Some people in life can be a bit negative and dour. That's definitely not the case with Stan. He was the first up every morning. He worked harder than anybody else and was physically always on the go. Despite his age, he would get stuck in with everything whether that be go kart racing or fire walking.

He was very good at giving you a different set of eyes. There were a couple of occasions where Stan's outside, mature experience was absolutely invaluable to the group.

Wayne Bennett has sometimes used older men in supporting roles, one such man being Ron Massey. He was Jack Gibson's right hand man and is in his eighties. He was a great coach forty years ago. Wayne Bennett is smart enough to realise that older people do have a bit to contribute. The game doesn't change that much really. More sports teams could embrace people like Stan even more.

Sometimes it was like having a wise granddad. He's seen all the troubles, sometimes we think we're the first generation to experience something but Stan had them all 30 or 40 years prior. Too many of us are wrapped up in our own importance to realise the value of older people around us.

I really valued Stan's contribution to what we did and I value my friendship with him very highly. I'm a big fan of his.

David Howes

I first came across Stan when I was at Rugby League Headquarters. Stan was one of the grade one referees at the time. We had what we called the Three Stooges because of their small height, there was Stan, Peter Massey and Vince Moss. They were all somewhat vertically challenged. I think they were chuffed about the Three Stooges nickname.

Stan's character came through in those days as we used to have long chats about the mines. His occupation came out in his refereeing as he had great attention to detail. His man management was excellent and his desire to do the job was high. Stan always made an impression at the RFL headquarters with the way he managed himself. The way he prepared and performed was exemplary.

Stan was one of the referees who gave a lot to his local referees' society as well. He didn't just strut around in his blazer; he put a lot back into his local area, bringing on the next generation of referees.

Our paths crossed again when I was appointed chief executive of Saints in 1995. At that time, and I think because of his mining background, Stan's view was that if he was employed somewhere, he would do everything he was asked to do no matter what it was. If he was given a job to do, he would do it well.

At the time, Stan was Eric Hughes' assistant and was doing all the video analysis for Eric. Regrettably, I took a little bit off him in one sense because we appointed Mike Gregory as assistant. Stan never took his bat home and kept smiling. I made his job bigger in other areas such as dealing with sponsors.

We were a full-time club for the first time and Stan became responsible for everything to do with equipment. The kitman title is a bit of a colloquialism. He became equipment manager which was more befitting the job that he actually did.

Saints had gone twenty years without winning a major trophy. They were reaching finals but never winning them. They were a club that had no idea what business they were doing or what money they had in the bank. It was a big board back then and slack would be the best word to describe them business wise. We tightened everything up and Stan bought into where we wanted to be.

Stan thought a lot about Eric who had been doing a good job, but we just felt we could improve by bringing in Shaun McRae. Stan could have easily left with Eric. He was loyal to the club and bought into the philosophy and culture we were trying to introduce.

Above all else, we wanted to win trophies and secondly, start making some money. Stan bought into that and all the changes we had to do.

I was very pleased and relieved that Stan stayed with the club. His role became a vital one for us. I'm a big believer in how you present yourself and people being in the right gear. We got a new deal with Mizuno within a year of being there. Stan came with us and attended all those meetings.

I like to think we took Stan on that journey of what we were trying to achieve. He was a major part of it. His attention to detail and his willingness to work to make sure things happened were great. The big thing in that role is to be ahead of yourself. Stan was always meticulous in how he prepared. He really bought into the fact that we were going to be a club that looked the part. I used to preach to the players that before they stepped off the coach, their tracksuits should be on properly. That's the first impression you make when you get off the bus, that you mean business.

Stan actively encouraged the whole culture of looking the part. His wife Celia is a lovely lady who has sacrificed some of her own leisure time for Stan because he's brought that much pleasure into the house. Members of his family would come and support Saints and support him.

When we achieved the success we did in 1996, the look on Stan's face and on other people there like Toffee Jack, Brian Collins, people who had been there a long time was fantastic. I'd never done club football before and Shaun was new to the head coach role. We both sat on the Wembley bus going through St Helens in the pouring rain on the day after we won the cup. The look on the St Helens peoples' faces and people like Stan showed they were living and loving the fact that we had won the trophy.

When I left Saints to go to Leeds, the Rugby Football League gave me the job as manager of England. Because I thought so highly of Stan, as soon as I sat down with the coach John Kear I told him I was putting my foot down, he could think about his assistant and his conditioner but I wanted Stan as my right hand man. Saints kindly released him for that six week period in 2000. He was in every planning and preparation meeting.

I did something deliberately when we were staying with Disney. We had been wearing a lot of Disney gear whilst over there. He had to issue Disney t-shirts and polo shirts. We then had Lincoln branded training gear for use when we got back to the UK. I knew Stan was in his hotel room sorting all this gear out. I also knew the players thought that all the kit arrived already bagged up for them. I'm not knocking the lads but they walk in and their meal is ready because the chef has done his job, the bus is ready because the driver has done his job. I deliberately brought the players in just as Stan was sorting all the kit. I saw one or two player's faces go "Shit" as it made them realise what a job Stan was doing for them.

One of the things of that World Cup was that we thanked everybody including ourselves, so if somebody volunteered to drive a minibus they'd get a round of applause. We thanked Disney, we thanked the staff. They all gave Stan a round of applause that day.

I would always get up early in the morning and me and Stan would have an hour together about half past six in the morning. We'd go for a walk together before starting work properly for the day. I thoroughly enjoyed that type of company as well as the rugby company.

Mike Forshaw

After Great Britain had drawn with New Zealand at the DW Stadium but won the series in 2002, Sean Long was getting dry after his shower, covered in his tattoos and his piercings. He had had his knob pierced and shouted to Stan about it, "What do you think about this?"

Stan just said, "There's only two types of men who have piercings down there, puffs and pirates and I can't see any galleons on the car park".

Jon Wilkin

Stan was a familiar face in a little room at the back of the old changing rooms at Knowsley Road. He had a cough that sounded like it was the remnants of someone who had been involved in the coal industry. Stan introduced himself to me. At that point, Stan used to mix our drinks and give us our fish oil tablets to take. I was new to all this so was taken aback to see Stan with a vat of sportsade, mixing it with a giant spoon, the coal dust cough being coughed over it.

He was a friendly face who had a story for everybody. If we turned up in a flash pair of boots, Stan would be there to tell you that it was just your uniform, your work overalls and that you shouldn't be bothered what it looks like. He would say he was never bothered what his helmet looked like down the pit. It was always funny having a bit of banter with Stan about stuff like that.

There was a period of time where we as players probably got pampered back, probably a lot more than we do now. That was down to Stan. You'd give him your boots after each training session and when you came back the next day, they would be cleaned. He'd know if the pitch was heavy and put your long studs in, or if the pitch was dry he'd put your short studs in. He'd wash your underpants or, in Wello's case, Stan would provide underpants.

Stan did a lot of the bits in the background that made training happen. Saints were doing it back then when a lot of other teams weren't. It was a real standout feature that you had a group of people headed up by Stan working hard behind the scenes for you.

Stan has good perspective on the game and on life from being a referee and working in Mines Rescue. He gives you an understanding of the real world and the pitfalls of life. Stan tells the younger players that he used to do all the things that they do. He reminds the younger guys how knowledgeable and wise he is.

As a young guy, I just used to take the opportunity to speak to Stan and just listen to him and his stories. He had such an interesting life and a great way of telling stories and passing on his wisdom. I really enjoyed listening to him. The more and more players who become full-time professionals, the more important people like Stan are.

Jamie Peacock

I always remember Stan wanting to be involved in everything. He always had an opinion on things. He always made sure that everything was right in the dressing room. Like all good kitmen, he had an opinion on rugby. The best ones are generally 97% right and Stan was one of those.

In the World Cup in 2000, it was my first time in the squad. We were trying to break down the barriers of being a new squad. We were sat in a small meeting room in our hotel and each of us had to get up in front of the group and tell them our best moment and our worst moment. Most players' worst moments were about not getting picked for a team. The best moments were winning a trophy; it was quite standard stuff for sportsmen. Stan got up and started telling us about his mining days and an occasion when men were trapped down the pit. It was his worst and best moment because some people had died but some got out alive. It put everything into perspective. That kind of lesson stood me in good stead because in the end, rugby is a game compared to something like that.

That was the best lesson I received off Stan, hearing about his personal tragedies and triumphs that far outweighed anything you could achieve in the game.

He is very approachable too. You often find that with the best people around clubs.